EVER LOYAL

The Biography of Neville Crump

TIM FITZGEORGE-PARKER

Stanley Paul
London Melbourne Auckland Johannesburg

Stanley Paul & Co. Ltd

An imprint of Century Hutchinson Ltd

62–65 Chandos Place, London WC2N 4NW

Century Hutchinson Australia (Pty) Ltd
PO Box 496, 16–22 Church Street, Hawthorn, Melbourne,
Victoria 3122, Australia

Century Hutchinson New Zealand Limited
PO Box 40-086 Glenfield, Auckland 10, New Zealand

Century Hutchinson South Africa (Pty) Ltd
PO Box 337, Bergvlei 2012, South Africa

First published 1987
© Tim Fitzgeorge-Parker 1987

Set in Linotron Sabon by
Rowland Phototypesetting Ltd, Bury St Edmunds, Suffolk
Printed in Great Britain by Redwood Burn Ltd,
Trowbridge, Wiltshire

ISBN 0 09 166190 0

Contents

Acknowledgements   vii
Introduction   1
Chapter One   3
         Two   9
         Three   27
         Four   59
         Five   77
         Six   84
         Seven   99
         Eight   109
         Nine   122
         Ten   132
         Eleven   139
         Twelve   151
         Thirteen   160
Index   177

Acknowledgements

I must express my warmest thanks to Lord Cadogan MC, a great friend and one of Neville Crump's principal owners, for encouraging me to write this book – in company with Colonel Simon Lycett-Green, Mr Arthur Thompson, Mr Gerry Scott and Neville's beloved daughter, Sarah, (Mrs Roger Walker). In addition I would like to thank John Penney for his help and for the use of his 'schoolboy' diary; the Editors of *Horse and Hound* and the *Sporting Life* for permission to quote John Oaksey and James Lambie; John Hislop for allowing me to quote him; and Neville Crump's great friend Shimi Lovat as well as his publishers, Weidenfeld and Nicholson, for passages from that magnificent book, March Past.

I am also most grateful to the very many people, friends and acquaintances of Neville and Brownie Crump who have allowed me to interview them for the purpose of this book.

Photographic acknowledgements

Thanks to Gerry Cranham and Sport and General for the use of their photographs.

''Unting fills my thoughts by day, and many a good run I have in my sleep. Many a dig in the ribs I gives Mrs J. when I think they're running into the warmint (renewed cheers). No man is fit to be called a sportsman wot doesn't kick his wife out of bed on a haverage once in three weeks.' (*John Jorrocks*)

R. S. Surtees

Introduction

On a cold January morning the gale-force wind blusters down from High Moor. Out of a leaden sky the sleet lashes the little North Yorkshire town of Middleham, battering the battlements of King Richard's ruined castle and the old brown buildings, sluicing down the broad main street. Up that street, heading for the moor, walks a string of powerful steeplechasers, night-capped and rugged, their helmeted stable lads leaning into the storm. The last horse carries a large ruddy-faced man in a saturated tweed cap and an army mackintosh. He looks part of the horse, in complete sympathy with the animal he loves so well. As he passes by sleepy, curtained windows, he shouts, 'Come on, you idle buggers! Get out of bed!' and then, in a cracked baritone, sensationally off key, he sings, 'Oh, what a beautiful morning, Oh what a beautiful day. . . .'

Punctual to the minute, as ever, our longest serving racehorse trainer, seventy-five-year-old Captain Neville Crump, the much loved hero of three Grand Nationals, is starting another day. And if his beloved daughter Sarah says with pride, 'Dad is eccentric, isn't he?', that is just an integral part of this great sportsman's wonderful character.

I

Neville Crump was born on 27 December 1910, the last of the great trainers to see the light of day in this vintage year which also produced Sir Noel Murless, Paddy Prendergast and Fulke Walwyn. Somewhat surprisingly for a Yorkshireman's grandson who was to spend most of his life in England's largest county, his birthplace was south of London, on the borders of Kent and Surrey, not far from Croydon, which has now been engulfed by the metropolis. This was his mother's country. She was a Mansell and her wealthy family lived in nearby Ashdown Forest.

Today, passing through the huge sprawling borough with a population of some 400,000, it is hard to believe that in the days before the First World War Croydon was still a small market town which had grown rapidly from a large village. Its subsequent growth has been faster than anywhere else, helped, of course, by the aerodrome, which, between the wars, was the forerunner of Heathrow. In the 1910s, however, despite the burgeoning housing estates and a great deal of game shooting in the area, there was still some reasonable foxhunting and Neville remembers hounds meeting at his home, Shortlands.

When he was five years old the Old Surrey Foxhounds amalgamated with the Burstow Park Harriers, which had been hunting foxes since 1866. So the first pack that Neville knew was the Old Surrey and Burstow Foxhounds.

Neville's wealthy Yorkshire grandfather, who was so keen on driving that he became a famous whip, was also so obsessed with gambling that, inevitably, he lost a fortune, which did not suit his son, Charles, Neville's father. Neville recalls, 'my old man did nothing but enjoy himself until he was about twenty-eight years old. Then, when his father went skint, he suddenly

3

realized that he would have to make his own way in the world. So he went to Australia and became a rancher for about eight years. But he became an even better horseman and loved every moment of it.

'He wouldn't have come home if he hadn't gone into a pub, picked up an old copy of the *Tatler* and seen that his sister was getting engaged to be married. This made him homesick and he returned to England, where he met my mother. He wanted to marry her, only to be told by her father in no uncertain terms, "Not bloody likely until you get yourself a job!"'

Fortunately Charles Crump was not only an outstanding horseman, but also a first-class mixer, as his son was later to become. 'He hunted regularly and became very friendly with some of the West Country farmers, one of whom asked him, "Can you sell my cheese?" "Anything you like," he said, "provided that you pay me!" So that's how he started. Soon he had his own cheese factory down in Wells, Somerset, making Cheddar cheese. In fact, he did so well that he was asked to be chairman of the Milk Marketing Board, but by then he was too old. He taught my old Mum to ride when she was about forty-five. I don't think she enjoyed it very much!'

Neville, however, started riding as soon as he could walk – on a donkey, led around by a nurse. These were the early days of motorcars, about which the donkey had some original ideas. 'I was warned off that flaming donkey, because, when a car came along, he would lie down in front of it! That winter for Christmas or my birthday two days later my Mum had bought me a beautiful white fur coat. When we met our first car the donkey lay down and rolled in the mud. So did I and so did the white fur coat. That was the end of my donkey riding!'

Neville's first school was at Limpsfield, between Reigate and Sevenoaks, where a former pupil was Arthur Carr, who captained Nottinghamshire and England and was a very fine cricketer. But already horses had taken over Neville's life and, at a very early age, accompanied by a groom, he started hunting with the Old Surrey and Burstow, whose country now embraced parts of Surrey, Sussex and Kent, adjacent to the Crawley and Horsham, Surrey Union, Southdown, West Kent and Eridge. Although it was not great hunting country, it provided a lot of fun for a small boy, learning to ride under the expert guidance of his father and the stud groom.

The famous artist, Cecil Aldin, at one time Master of the South Berks, wrote of the Home Counties:

> These bad hunting countries are better for boys and girls to take their first lessons in hunting than the crowded fields of Leicestershire. Here they can see and hear what hounds are doing and can often see them hunt. They are great schooling grounds for the children, because they teach them to use their eyes and ears as well as their riding muscles. Every time give me a provincial country for the Young Entry; their schooling ground for Leicestershire.

Of his father's many good friends, Sam Marsh, a superb horseman-dealer ('The ladies, God bless 'em!') and one of the old school of professional horsemasters who are sadly an extinct species, perhaps had most influence on the boy. 'Sam came to my christening. He was a great friend of my old man and together we became very friendly with the Askews.'

The Askews were a family of considerable substance who lived near Redhill. They were closely related to the Ranks, the famous sporting millers, whose racehorses were to become household names in the succeeding years. The Askews collected some fine point-to-pointers, including a top-class performer called Leconfield. The time to back him was when the eldest son Gerald was prevented from riding and Sam Marsh substituted.

Neville was eight years old when the war ended and the annual point-to-points fired the spark of racing that has never grown dim. But even before that the proximity of Gatwick, then one of the finest racecourses in the country, flat and National Hunt, was perhaps even more inflammatory, showing the small boy a glimpse of even greater things in the racing world.

In 1915 guns were blasting holes in a generation across the Channel and critics of the war effort were indignant that racing could continue on the slogan 'Business as usual'. Others considered sport to be as important to morale as theatres and music halls. The generals and admirals told the politicians that Napoleon had said, 'The moral is to the physical as two is to one.' So uniforms lucky enough to be on leave on National day splashed patches of khaki and navy blue in the Aintree crowd, as Ally Sloper, trained by Aubrey Hastings, won to make Lady Nelson the first woman to own the winner since the great chase was inaugurated in 1837.

It was a perilous ride for Jack Anthony. He was nearly down at the second, saved only by his brother Ivor, who was upsides on Ilston. As Fred Rimell was to do for Bruce Hobbs twenty-three years later, Ivor reached out, grabbed his brother by the breeches and dragged him back into the saddle.

At the Canal ditch Ally Sloper blundered again and Jack was between his ears. But on the second circuit the six-year-old settled down, jumping sensibly and keeping up such a determined gallop that he was overhauling Jacobus at the last. He cleared the fence the better and ran away to win from Jacobus, with Father Confessor third.

Until Lady Nelson's success only three women had ever owned a National runner. None had ever looked like winning until Lady Nelson paid £700 for a brown horse by Travelling Lad, which had earlier been sold at Doncaster for just 25 guineas. The victory was in key with the campaign for equality for women. Forty-five years later, after another great war, Neville would be adding to the success of women in the world's greatest steeplechase.

At the end of 1915 Aintree was taken over by the War Office and closed to racing. The National was transferred to Gatwick and called 'the Racecourse Association Steeplechase' with the prize reduced to £500. It was won by Vermouth. In 1917 the name was again changed, to the War National Steeplechase, and was won by Ballymacad, the third of Aubrey Hastings's record four-timers. Stablemate Ally Sloper was third.

The last substitute National was the first race that seven-year-old Neville ever watched and it was the best of the three. It was a typical National romance, enough to inspire any boy with sporting inclinations, with which young Crump's head was already full.

Poethlyn was foaled in 1910, the same year in which Neville was born. Bred in Cheshire by Major Hugh Peel, Poethlyn was sold as a weak, sickly yearling to a Shrewsbury hotelier for £7. The following year Hugh Peel bought the horse back for £50 and gave him to his wife. Poethlyn took some time to reach maturity and it may not have been unfortunate that the war interrupted his early career. In all he won fifteen races and, during the seasons 1918–19 was unbeaten in ten, including the Prince of Wales Chase, Sandown, the Lancashire Chase twice, each time carrying 12 stone, and the Grand National twice. It was a never-to-be-forgotten thrill for Neville to see this great horse, ridden by Lester Piggott's grandfather, Ernie Piggott, carrying 11 st 6 lb to victory over Captain Dreyfus and Ballymacad.

By the following April the war was over and the National returned to its rightful home. Men celebrated their release from trench, destroyer and merchant ship by rushing to Aintree for a race which seemed to stand for England in a shattered world. It was a race which the favourite had to win, and mighty Poethlyn duly obliged, joining the elite who had won in successive years, sharing with Cloister, Jerry M and Manifesto the distinction of winning under 12 st 7 lb.

From Limpsfield Neville graduated to a preparatory school called Hazelwood and then, at the age of twelve, to Marlborough, where his companions included John Hunt, later to be knighted as the famous explorer of Everest fame. 'I didn't reckon much on him,' says Neville. 'In fact, I thought he was a sod because he never stopped beating me!'

Another well-known Marlburian a few years earlier was Colonel 'Squeak' Thompson, later to become a great friend of Neville and a stalwart of the National Hunt scene. He told Neville once, 'We have one thing in common. We were both in the bottom form at Marlborough all the time we were there!' 'That's not quite true,' Crump replied, 'because you were slung out!'

Neville recalls, 'He was, too. My father had more bloody sense. He went to the headmaster and said, "This is a pretty bloody bad school. If you don't get my son through his exams,

I'm not paying you any fees. You get him through." So they didn't sling me out and somehow I got into Oxford – to Balliol, too!'

By this time, in the late twenties, the family had moved from Surrey to a charming house in a village called North Stoke, near Wallingford in the south Oxfordshire country. 'Super house, sweet little place. The old man was there until the Second World War.'

2

The mention of Balliol has always conjured up thoughts of brains and classical scholars, which invariably amuses the undergraduate of 1928. 'All the others who went to Balliol with me got honours and I only got a pass. Bloody lucky to get that, too.

'After a year we had to pass our first exam. Of course, I failed. So I was had up by the Master of Balliol, who told me that I'd have to leave the place – go down. So I said, "That's all right, sir, I'll have to go down. But it just so happens that I'll be rowing for the college at Henley this summer." "Good God!" he said. "You're not quite as stupid as I thought you were. You'd better stay on a bit longer!"

'When I finally left Balliol with a pass degree I wasn't very popular. I should have done better.'

These were unreal days midway between the two world wars. Against a background of industrial depression there was a gaiety, natural to the well-breeched young like Neville, but forced on their elders, who, while trying to recapture the joys of their pre-1914 youth, knew in their hearts that it was ephemeral, that Armageddon lay just around the corner. They blinded themselves to the cracks in the ice. Imagining that they could still recapture the golden age, the skaters whirled even more furiously than before, trying to convince themselves that it would last, but knowing full well that it would not. However, those who played out the charade would never forget it. Whatever and whoever else might die, they would retain memories of those golden days.

Neville's sporting life blossomed at Oxford, particularly when his father became Master of the South Oxfordshire Foxhounds. Recently absorbed into the Vale of Aylesbury, this country, which lay in Oxfordshire and Buckinghamshire, was about eighteen miles north to south and fifteen miles in greatest width from east to west. On the north it adjoined the Bicester; on the west the Old Berkshire and the Heythrop; on the south the Garth and South Berks; and, on the east the OBH. It provided good sport, if well hunted.

It was hardly surprising that Neville failed his exams. 'I did a lot of hunting and point-to-pointing while I was up at Oxford,' he says. 'Lord Rosebery's son was up at the same time and he won the first race I ever rode in. Old Harry Rosebery himself was Master of the Whaddon Chase at the time and a very good friend of my father. He was a great sport and did a lot for us. A little later, when I joined the Army, he asked my father, "Why doesn't Neville hunt with us?" When my old man said that I couldn't afford it, Harry Rosebery said, "Of course he can. He won't have to pay anything." So I used to go out on an old troop horse and had great times. He was very good to me.'

Oxford in 1930, both town and gown, was less than half her present size. Despite a war which had killed so many of her former undergraduates, the flower of their country, she remained the same as when Matthew Arnold had written more than half a century earlier: 'And that sweet City with her dreaming spires, She needs not June for beauty's heightening.'

Oxford University was still a male preserve with absent-minded dons who wrote fine whodunnit novels. It was dominated by privilege and class structure but was still blissfully unaware that there was anything wrong with this system. Universal television, Women's Lib and the permissive society were still a quarter of a century ahead on the other side of a Second World War, which was destined to shake British civilization to its roots.

Little had changed since a future Prime Minister, Harold Macmillan, now Lord Stockton, an Eton and Balliol scholar, wrote shortly before the First World War,

Thro' Balliol eyes there were no women; ours was an entirely masculine – almost monastic – society. We knew, of course, that there were female students and that their colleges were situated on the suburban periphery. They never came in to our rooms and they played no part in our lives. They were not, I think, full members of the University and they joined no political societies. Nor were they members of the Union. If they came to lectures, they were escorted by a duenna.

There was very little mixing of the sexes. During the term the female undergraduates remained secluded in their colleges. Those men rich enough to own fast cars could drive up to London for dates. For the majority a train, known as the Flying Fornicator, left Paddington at 10.40 p.m. to bring undergraduates back into college before lock-up at midnight. It was not easy to get a twenty-four-hour pass. At Oxford today such a thing is no longer required.

Bernard Shaw wrote: 'Very nice sort of place Oxford I should think for people that like that sort of place.' Many young men on the threshhold of life did like that sort of place. There were plenty of parties. One night Neville went to a big party at Magdalen. Walking back over Magdalen Bridge in his dinner jacket while the milkman was doing his rounds, he was dared by a friend, 'Come on, you silly soft sod, you can't walk along that parapet!'

'Of course I bloody well can,' said Neville. He got up on the parapet and went straight over into the river. The Isis was good and deep and he had to swim. When he eventually emerged soaking and looked for the man who had made the dare, he had vanished. 'I never found him!' he says. 'That was Shimi.'

He made a great many friends during his time at Oxford, including a very special one, Shimi Lovat, the same Lord Lovat who was to become the great Commando leader in ten years' time. A few years ago at York races Neville was hailed by a large handsome man from the top of the stands: 'Cor, bloody hell, not you!' Neville looked up smiling. Then Shimi yelled at the top of his voice, 'Have you given up all forms of sexual intercourse?' Neville shouted back, 'Oh yes' to receive the reply, 'That's why you look so bloody horrible!' 'Who's that common man?' someone asked. 'That happens to be the 17th Lord Lovat!' Neville replied.

Sport was at a premium at Oxford in those days and most of the undergraduates were supremely fit. Neville was a good oar, rowing for his college and, of course, did a lot of hunting, racing and point-to-pointing. He, Shimi and a number of their friends also enjoyed the Oxford University Cavalry Squadron, the mounted branch of the Officers' Training Corps (OTC), which was known affectionately as the Irregular Whores and had a long line of candidates waiting to enlist.

In the early morning during the summer term weekly training took place on Port Meadow. The cadets were mounted on long-suffering hirelings, kept in livery stables, which were hunted with foxhounds and drag hounds throughout the winter. Neville, who was an under officer while Shimi Lovat was a sergeant, was better off. As his father was Master of the South Oxfordshire Hounds, he was able to mount himself on hunt servants' horses, which were properly trained to go across country.

The rough-riding sergeant major was Percy Rhimes of the 16th/5th Lancers, a regular NCO of the finest kind, hard as nails with a caustic wit. He was an outstanding instructor and was to become a legend in the university. Percy Rhimes joined in plenty of parties, but woebetide the recruits the following morning who had had a skinful the night before. With vindictive glee Rhimes would shout, 'Ride, quit and cross your stirrups. Ride, trot!' Round and round the recruits would go with Rhimes apparently completely unmoved by the agony they were beginning to suffer. This sadistic practice is remembered in the old cavalry recruits' song:

> Sergeant, sergeant, oh give my stirrups to me to me,
> Sergeant, sergeant, give back my stirrups to me.
> I've stuck it for one bloody hour,
> I've stuck it as long as I could,
> I've stuck it for one bloody hour,
> My arsehole is not made of wood!

Camps at Tidworth and Aldershot, where cadets lived as troopers, sleeping with their saddles, six to a tent beside the horse lines, keeping their own mess (only cadets without cars ever dined there) were tremendous fun. Members of the regular Cavalry Division were unfailingly kind to the OTC, and colonels with an eye on the future young entry saw to it that the Oxford University Cavalry Squadron got baths in barracks, dined with their future regiments and were asked to all the polo and cricket parties on Saturday afternoons. Nevertheless the training programme was good and tough. There was no quarter given. It was a case of work hard and play hard.

Neville says, 'The most amusing incident that I can remember was the 1930 camp at Tidworth. A good few of us went to the Queen's Bay's sergeants' mess and, not unnaturally, got very drunk. On the way back to camp we passed the tented camp of the Sandhurst cadets, and somehow or other Shimi Lovat and I managed to get into one of the tents. Unfortunately, being extremely inebriated, we did not realize that there was a body in a camp bed which we turned upside down to find a sword, which Shimi promptly drew and stuck through the bed. We looked up to find a red hat hanging on a peg, "Christ," I said, "this must be the Brigadier!" We ran as fast as we could back to our lines. The next morning there was an identity parade, but the Brigadier failed to recognize us, which was lucky, and we escaped with a hell of a ticking off.

'Many years later I reminded Shimi of the night when he nearly did irreparable damage to a senior officer by sticking the sword between the Brigadier's legs!'

In his fascinating memoir, *March Past**, Shimi Lovat wrote:

> The *armée blanche* has gone for ever. People still talk about the 'Cavalry spirit' without knowing exactly what it means. That indefinable quality is not easily recognized except in barracks or on active service; then it can lift a regiment and inspire ordinary men. But I will venture a definition of its basic principles: fight hard, play hard and take what's coming – laughter or tears!

There were from time to time gallops across country over formidable obstacles which resulted in some crashing falls and were apt to be won by the man who was to train three Grand National winners. Even then Neville was a first-class horseman and knew not the meaning of fear. Already the amazing Crump wit, which was to become such a byword in the world

---

* March Past (Weidenfeld & Nicholson, 1978).

of racing that the very mention of his name brings a smile to every face, was beginning to make its presence felt.

This was never better illustrated than by the following story which Shimi Lovat, with the aid of an eyewitness, tells. Remember that the period was halfway between the two world wars and many of the cadets, knowing that another war was inevitable, were, like Neville and Shimi, about to enter the regular army and anything remotely Germanic was extremely unpopular. Moreover, the richest undergraduates at the time were mostly foreigners. Shimi wrote:

A night on the tiles, but farther afield, proved the downfall of another member of the Squadron. The Baron – we never caught his real name; it sounded like the Vicomte de Broncoute – was of Belgian extraction. A stout, bespectacled individual of Teutonic mien, he was immediately dubbed 'Baron Von Braunshnaut'. The nobleman, who had few friends, was anathema to Sergeant Rhimes and a goldmine to the grooms. He had an arrogant conceit. That he was well equipped was reluctantly accepted; that his horse was a superior type of Hanoverian, with impeccable manners and certain dressage ability, could not be denied; but in camp such niceties were considered superfluous. The retainer with a cockade in his hat, left behind at Oxford, was replaced by the bookie's runner. The Baron understood the finer points of *haute école* (having won prizes in *concours hippiques* on the Continent), but his style of riding did not appeal to Percy Rhimes, whose scathing comments seared like fire:

'You must sit down in the saddle, sir, if you want to join those Death's Head Hussars. Don't lean forward, sir. Quit and cross your stirrups, sir. Now trot and sit straight. Fold your arms, sir; grip with your knees, head up, heels down, toes out! You will sit correctly if it takes all day to teach you, sir. Are you married, sir? I'm afraid you will be disappointed, sir, if you sit on them, sir! Remember our nursery rhyme for beginners, sir!

"With your head and your heart held high
Your heels and your hands kept low;
With your legs gripped tight to your horse's sides
And your elbows close to your own."'

The Baron did not like such pleasantries – still less having a strip torn off him by an NCO. When he showed signs of blowing his top with the rough-rider, Neville Crump, recently promoted to Under Officer and a good horseman, took charge. He disliked the Baron on the grounds that he had kicked his father's hounds and had never apologized. He fairly mobbed him up. 'Do you know Sevenoaks, Braunshnaut?' Sullenly the Baron nodded in assent. 'Then stuff five of them up your arse. Did that hurt, trooper?' A shocked silence. 'Well, in that case, stuff the other two up! That should straighten you in the saddle.'

It was an episode in the Long Valley which proved the Baron's undoing. This is what happened, as described by an eyewitness: 'The Oxford University Cavalry Squadron was about to mount, but the call "Boots and Saddles" found Von Braunshnaut unprepared. Tubbs, waiting with his horse, inquired anxiously for the "foreign gentleman", for names were quite beyond him.

'Just at the off, the gallant horseman, who had been in London overnight, appeared and mounted in hot haste, but failed to notice that the girth needed adjustment. Officer cadets in theory saddled their own chargers, but the rich and lazy chaps often paid the grooms to do it for them. Gathering up the reins he cantered off, despite shouts of warning from the stablemen.

'Once formed up, the Oxford Cavalry proceeded at a trot to join the big parade in the Long Valley, where General Blakiston Houston was to review the troops. The regiments rode past: at a trot, canter and finally at gallop. In this last manoeuvre the Oxford Cavalry followed the Life Guards; behind them thundered two lancer regiments. It was a brave show and the horses enjoyed it as much as the men who rode them. At middle pace the band played us by to "The Irish Washer Woman", then disaster struck!

'The Baron was not far in front of me and I saw his saddle begin to turn. He made a gallant effort to stay on board and Oliver Woods and Bailey, a powerful New Zealander from Magdalen, edged forward to catch him, but to no avail. His saddle slipped and the Baron bit the dust! Two rocking, galloping regiments rode over him. Above the thunder of the charge came the cool voice of Percy Rhimes, our peerless instructor; "Keep your head under your saddle, sir. The Seventh Hussars are close behind."

'At the end of the parade the Reverend Tubbs approached me in the horse-lines; he looked worried, for the Baron was a good customer. "Where has he got to, sir?" he asked hoarsely. "What's left of him is down in the Long Valley" came the callous reply. "You'd better take a cab and pick up the bits."

'The unfortunate Continental finally limped in bruised and minus his hat, and immediately had his name taken for being improperly dressed, "Where's your Service Dress cap?" inquired Neville. The Baron was incensed. "Up your arse!" came the swift riposte! Braunshnaut was learning fast; even so Crump got the better of him.

'Charged next morning, at Adjutant's Orders, with loss of army equipment, the Baron's parting shot told against him. Now he faced two offences under various Army Acts:

1. Returning improperly dressed from the Major-General's Inspection.
2. Failing to report the loss of Government Property – one service dress cap.

'Neville supplied the details: "On being questioned where he had put this article of clothing, the officer cadet replied "Up your arse, schweinhund" or words to that effect. I immediately took his name for making a statement that I knew to be false, and placed him on the Charge Sheet, sir." The Baron was ordered to make good the deficiency.'

By now Neville was point-to-pointing regularly every season. He recalls, 'My first memory of riding a race was at my father's South Oxfordshire point-to-point, on a horse which he had bought from Peter Thrale, a first-class vet and trainer. The Prince of Wales, later to become King Edward VIII, rode in the same race. When we changed in the tent, nobody would go and sit next to him because they were too shy. Someone told me, "Go on! You're the Master's son. Go and sit next to him." So I did and he was terribly nice to me. We seemed to have a lot to talk about and were chatting away when he said, "What's the matter with all those stupid buggers over there?" I said, "I think they are all a bit frightened of you, sir. Like me." The Prince of Wales was quite upset. "Oh knickers!" he said. He was very keen but sadly he wasn't a very good jockey and they had to stop him riding, for fear that he would hurt himself.'

When he was about to leave Oxford Neville's father decided that he should go into the Army. After his experience with the Oxford University Cavalry Squadron and, bearing in mind that his whole life was already bound up with horses, Neville said, 'All right. Put me in the Cavalry.' His father said, 'No, I can't afford that.' So Neville refused to join the Army.

But by then he had made friends with John de Moraville, later to become a successful trainer, but now in the 4th Hussars. He asked Neville, 'Where are you going when you leave Oxford?' and when Neville told him that he had no idea, John asked, 'Would you like to join my regiment, the 4th Hussars?' Neville said, 'Yes, why not?' John promised to talk to his commanding officer and Neville found himself joining the 4th Hussars.

One of Neville's many Oxford friends was Chris Johnston, older brother of Brian Johnston, the well-known BBC cricket commentator. Like Brian, Chris had been to Eton before going to University. He too wanted to join a cavalry regiment. Neville recalls, 'Both of us had behaved very badly at Oxford. We were going for an interview with an old general of whom we were terrified. On the way we had quite a few drinks and in the taxi Chris said, "God I've got to have a piss!" I said, "Well, you can't piss here." He said, "Oh yes I can," knelt down in the back of the taxi, and did it there and then. I thought, If the General saw that you wouldn't get into the Cavalry! When we got out I said, "I hope the man in the front did not see." Whereupon the taxi driver said to Chris, "You dirty bastard!" So I said, "For Christ sake, give him a couple of quid and keep him quiet!" We went in to the interview and after talking to us and looking up our case histories, the General said, "All right, you boys. We'll take you in the Army, but one goes in one regiment and one goes in another. You're not going in together!"'

So young Neville came down from Oxford and set about collecting his uniform and kit to join the 4th Hussars, who had returned from a spell of duty in India and were now stationed in the famous cavalry barracks at York.

Getting equipped to join a cavalry regiment in those days was quite a performance and involved a tremendous amount of expense. The army allowed the princely sum of £60 as a uniform and kit allowance. As a pair of Maxwell polo boots or field boots with trees cost 15 guineas and you needed at least four pairs of them, it was obvious that a great deal of money would have to be found by the parents of the young officer. Moreover all uniform had to come from the prescribed tradesmen, who were always the most expensive. For example, boots had to be made by Maxwell or, possibly, Peal; breeches, of which you needed several pairs, had to be tailored by Huntsman or Tautz; and caps had to come from Herbert Johnson or Lock, depending on which hatter was the regimental choice. Even shirts had to be hand-made!

The young officer needed at least two service dress jackets cut and furnished in regimental style and two pairs of khaki slacks to go with them. He needed blue patrols, with both overalls sporting the wide yellow cavalry stripe, patent boots and spurs as well as blue slacks, complete mess kit with blue coat and gold braid, and in those days it was often necessary to have full-dress uniform for parades. All these had to be made by the regimental tailor, who was normally either Huntsman or Rogers. It was never necessary to move far away from Savile Row to get oneself fitted out.

Beautifully engraved cavalry officers' swords came from Wilkinson's, now famous as the makers of razorblades. So did the zinc-lined uniform trunks, Sam Browne belts, revolver holsters, spurs and camping equipment. Nothing was standard. Nothing was the same as the kit used by other regiments. Every regiment had its own individual pattern. Therein, of course, lay the expense.

When having a pair of boots and breeches made, the procedure was, first, to visit Huntsman and Maxwell. After your measurements had been taken and the work started, you returned for a first fitting. The young officer would go to Huntsman, where he would put on a pair of breeches, held together with cotton tacks, and in these he would hobble out to a taxi to take him the short distance to Maxwell's, where boots, in a similar state of unreadiness, would be placed upon his feet and legs for him to return for adjustments to Huntsman. In the end, of course, the result was magnificent, but the cost was prohibitive. Even in those days there would be little, if any, change out of £1000.

Each cavalry regiment was like a club. It was a collection of comfortably off young men who liked each other's company but were also individuals. The fact that they had to have private means was in practice a very good thing. It meant that, if the men under their command should be unfairly treated by higher authority, they were independent enough to stand up for them, even if it meant risking their commission. Many an officer has resigned from the Army because he felt that his soldiers were being unfairly treated.

In the horse days an officer was always given the maximum amount of leave, provided that he was going to spend it in the pursuits of which his commanding officer approved, preferably racing, hunting or polo. There were two results of this. First, although the phrase 'Carry on, Sergeant Major' has been misused and abused by many people from other walks of life, jealous of the Cavalry, the Guards and other crack regiments, in fact it concealed a remarkable asset of those regiments over other units. A cavalry officer, however young he might be, however blasé he might appear, had to know every facet of his job from A to Z, and he had to have that rare characteristic of leadership. Otherwise he would quietly find himself seconded to another branch of the Army.

When such a leader was away, his NCOs ran the show and naturally, in the normal course of events, became more and more skilful at doing so. It was they who had to impose the discipline. Just as a good huntsman never rates his own hounds, but leaves it to the whippers-in, so that the pack adore their boss, so when the officer came back from leave, always assuming that he was up to the exacting standard required, he was the unquestioned leader of a well-drilled team.

When it came to mechanization, the horsed cavalry soldier, however humble, had immense advantages over his counterpart who had been brought up from the word go in a tank regiment. The latter, whether he had been a driver, a lap gunner or a wireless operator, had been encased in layers of armour, unable to see anything except, at best, a very limited view. In contrast, the trooper on a horse has, from a very early age, to guide something other than himself. Sometimes he may be employed as squadron galloper, in which case he has to take a message from his own squadron leader and find his way across country to the commanding officer of another squadron to deliver his message. He has to guide not only himself, but also his horse, examining the terrain to find the best way to take. The bond of the horse that exists between officers, NCOs and men is the secret why all cavalry regiments were such happy families and why they were able to work together in that perfect combination that makes for efficiency.

Standing in stables for an hour and a half, superintending, while the men, stripped to the waist in the summer months and as fit as could be, groomed, watered and fed the horses, or discussing the problems of troop horse B 32's ringworm, B 48's rubbed tail, B 29's failure to put on flesh and B 3's bloody-minded refusal ever to leave the ranks, the young officer got to know his men personally. When that same B 3, bloody-minded as ever, kicked Trooper MacTavish in a very tender portion of his anatomy and the soldier in a moment of blind fury kicked him back, the officer understood and sympathized. When, on riding school, he saw the same Trooper MacTavish put on the floor three times and still get up smiling, he would say to himself, 'Well, he may have a quick temper, but by God, he's got guts – and that's the sort of man I want.'

It was the same from the NCO's and others' point of view. They saw their spotty-faced young troop officer play a really dashing game of polo or ride a stinking horse bravely in to the last fence in a race as though the obstacle were not there and they went away to adjust their first impressions of him. Thanks to the horse, the officers were not dolled-up figureheads, whom the trooper must salute whatever his opinion of them; nor were the troopers just a troop of permanent nuisances, whose health and comfort was the curse of the officer's life. They knew each other, respected each other and were friends.

When Neville joined the 4th Hussars in York he was welcomed not only by John de Moraville but also, in particular, by Peter Dollar, one of the more popular officers. 'Hell of a good chap,' says Neville. 'Only died recently. He was a right old spiv really! When I joined, I learned that his father had owned most of the horse cabs in London. Peter's brother Graham was in the Carabiniers – a terrific man, who could do anything with a horse. He ran the trick ride in his regiment and could make a horse lie down, sit down, stand up, do anything. When I had to run my musical ride he came and told me how to do it. Peter didn't like hunting, but he was mad about polo and brilliant at it. I didn't like polo. He said to me once, "You ride well. Why don't you play polo?" and I said, "Apart from anything else I can't afford it." It cost a fortune to play.'

The 4th Hussars remained in York for only about a week after Neville joined and then moved to Colchester. The whole regiment – 600 horses and 900 men – travelled by train. By today's standards this would seem to be a Herculean task. But in the 1930s it was normal to travel horses by train and to water them at various stops along the line. The rolling stock was designed for the transportation of horses, and before, during and in the years immediately after the war the most valuable yearlings in the world were transported from Doncaster Sales to Newmarket and Lambourn in this extremely safe way.

Every cavalry officer had two servants: the first servant (known in every other branch of the army as a batman) looked after his officer's clothing and general equipment, keeping him, as it were, on the road at all times; the second servant looked after the officer's two chargers and his own troop horse. He was responsible, of course, for the state of the officer's tack, ensuring that, when they went on parade, the horse was as well turned out as the rider.

Soon after Neville joined he was awakened to the stark realities of life when his second servant, a deeply religious man, complained to him that he had been sexually assaulted by an officer. 'That really shook me,' said Neville. 'I thought, This is a bloody game! I had to report the matter to my Senior Officer, David Harrison, who referred the matter to the colonel, and for about a month the officer concerned was confined to his quarters under close arrest and at all times a subaltern had to be on duty looking after him. Not a very happy state of affairs.

I believe the chap became a very famous doctor, but I never saw him again!'

Every day one subaltern would be detailed to perform the duties of orderly officer. His term of duty lasted twenty-four hours and during that time he had to be constantly available. He would inspect the soldiers' meals, asking if they had any complaints, and would always be at the adjutant's disposal. It was not a particularly popular duty and, if a young officer misbehaved in any way he would be punished by being given extra stints as orderly officer. If you were lucky enough to have a fellow subaltern who was particularly lazy or in some other way merited punishment, you were in clover. He might be made orderly officer for a week or a fortnight, which would mean that his brother officers were excused duty for that period of his sentence.

One of the orderly officer's more tiresome duties was, after dinner at night, making a tour of inspection of the stables and of the barrackrooms where the soldiers slept to make sure that all was well. At Colchester the traditional cavalry barracks had stable blocks wherein the horses were tied up in stalls. It was not a bad practice, whatever people may tell you today. The late, great Atty Persse told me, 'I kept some of my best racehorses in stalls. Bachelor's Double, for example, was never in a loose box. The advantage is that they can't walk about and lose condition. After all, they are not human beings, and what more can they want than to have their food, hay and water, and be able to lie down whenever they want to in a nice soft bed?' The disadvantage, from the orderly officer's point of view (and also from that of the troop horses) was that on the night before a big parade, when it was important for them to be spotlessly clean the next day, lying down in their bedding, frequently on dung, was not a good thing. Therefore, when the orderly officer went round stables at about 11 o'clock at night, he was liable to find all the light-coloured – particularly the grey – horses tied up short so that they could not lie down. Administering a blistering rocket to the trooper who was on stable guard, the officer would order the knots to be untied so that the animals had plenty of freedom to lie down. He knew perfectly well that, as soon as he left the stable, the stable guard would be tying them up on the short rack again.

While at Colchester Neville tried playing polo but he was not particularly successful, and he instead concentrated on hunting and point-to-pointing as well as a little show jumping. History was created in one particular point-to-point back in his old Surrey country. 'I found myself in the same race as Ryan Price, who was a brilliant horseman and a top-class point-to-point rider. I should have known better. I came up on his inside and he tried to push me through the wing. So I did the same to him. We had a fairly rough race, which eventually I won. In the changing room Ryan came up and said, "You bastard! Where have you come from?" I said, "You don't call me a bastard!" We were pushing each other and were just about to get stuck in – he would have killed me, he was much better than me – when a Steward stepped in between us and said, "Hey, steady, you boys!" Ryan shook my hand and said, "Oh, come on, my friend," and we were friends ever after!'

Ryan Price rode over a hundred point-to-point winners before becoming one of the bravest and toughest of the Commando officers during the war, and then a champion National Hunt trainer, winning every worthwhile race including the Grand National, the Champion Hurdle, and the Gold Cup. Like Neville, he was to become a legend in his own lifetime.

I asked Neville whether when riding in all these point-to-points and races under Rules he had broken many bones. He laughed and said, 'I must have done because a few years ago I went to a hospital up here in Yorkshire, run by Catholic priests, to discover whether a pain in my chest meant that I had heart trouble. They X-rayed me and the old priest couldn't believe it. "Have you seen your ribs?" Of course I said no, and he told me, "You haven't got one that hasn't been cracked! That's what's the matter with you. You have one there which hasn't mended properly and you have adhesions – go home and don't worry about it. You'll be all right." So I must have had a few cracks.'

Neville completed an eighteen month course at the Cavalry

School, Weedon, and then rejoined the Regiment at Aldershot. Like all young officers, he had to go through sword drill dismounted on the square. His instructor was Sergeant Major 'Dickie' Bird, a soldier of the old school, who had been a bookmaker's clerk in civvy street. Although he stood no nonsense, he was scrupulously fair and immensely popular.

Neville recalls, 'John de Moraville had a topping little horse which he had bought from Weedon for £40. He had been a demonstration horse and you could buy them out in those days when they became too old. John had given up riding and had asked me to pilot the horse for him in the regimental race, which, of course, I won because this was a super animal. Our Colonel, old Scotty Cockburn, got hold of John and said, "I'm glad your horse won but I think it is disgraceful that you let that young boy ride him. Why didn't you ride him yourself?" "Well," said John, "I gave the matter considerable thought and decided that it was about time I gave up the pigskin for the bottle!"

'Then I won the open race the next day on the same horse, so we all went up to London. Stephen Eve, who was later to be my best man and who had joined a year after me, was in the party and we all decided to have a tremendous celebration after winning these two races. On the way home Crump, considering himself the hero of the day, insisted on driving. I went up on the pavement and everywhere. Eventually they made me get out and Stevie drove. We got as far as Hounslow where the Carabiniers were stationed and I was putting my head out of the car and shouting and making a general nuisance of myself when a policeman came along. He said, "Come on. I want you all to come to the station to see if you can walk a straight line." Then he said to me, "I don't want you" and kicked me straight between the legs and pushed me out on to the pavement. We went to the police station, where Steve somehow walked the line and got away with it. They couldn't do much with us – it was lucky they did not have breathalysers in those days – so we went back to the car. They pushed us in and as I got into the car I got a kick up the backside from the policeman's big boot.

"Get in, you bastard!" he said. He laughed himself silly when I landed bang on my head.

'I was quite incapable of driving. We ended up in a night club and eventually Steve got us home. The following morning, not unnaturally, I was feeling terrible. We were doing sword drill on the square and when we returned our swords to their scabbards we were supposed to get them in first time. This particular morning Sergeant Major Bird was getting increasingly fed up with me. He had been through all the usual corny exhortations like, "Come on, sir! You'd get it in quick enough if it had a bit of hair round it!" But I still couldn't get the sword in. In the end I slung it on the floor. Dickie Bird came up menacingly. "Now, Mr Crump, sir. That wasn't very clever, sir. Pick it up, sir," and as I bent to pick it up he said, "Pick it up, you horrible little bastard, or I'll——!" I'll never forget that. It was terrible!

'Anyway, when it was all over Dickie Bird came up and said, "Come on. You're not feeling very well. We'll go into the sergeants' mess." I admitted, "Yes, it's horrible, Sergeant Major." He said, "You look bloody horrible too." So we went into the sergeants' mess and by the time we left I was nearly as bad as I had been the night before.'

Every year each cavalry regiment had a horse inspection by the General Officer Commanding. The officer who had the best squadron or the best troop got the glory. Shortly after this episode, when he had made a great friend of Sergeant Major Bird, who was supervising the squadron parade, Neville stood, watching his troop go by. 'I thought I had seen one of the horses before and muttered something to Dickie Bird. "Shut up!" he said. Afterwards, when my troop had won and we had adjourned to the sergeants' mess for a celebratory drink, I told Dickie Bird that I thought that two or three of the horses must have been round twice. "Of course," he said. "All our thin ones went to the veterinary lines and I let the fat ones go round twice!"' In a few years' time Neville was to meet Dickie Bird again.

Despite his denials Neville was now becoming a good cavalry officer. As long as the regiment had horses, he loved every moment of it. But Neville had no time for mechanization and he decided he wanted to leave the Army. One afternoon in 1935 Neville was having a sleep. 'I had been up at six o'clock in the morning, riding work,' he says, 'so it seemed the sensible thing to do. There was a knock on the door, it was the Brigadier, Lord Willoughby Norrie. "So that's how you spend your afternoons?" he said. "No wonder you don't want to stay in the bloody army!" "Sorry, General," I said. "Don't keep calling me General," he said. "Come and have a talk. I've been wanting to see you."

'I told him, "I didn't join the Army to drive around in these tanks. I joined the Army to go hunting and enjoy myself!" So he asked, "What would you like to do?" and I said, "I'd like to train racehorses, but I can't get out of the Army. You're the only person who can get me out." He said, "Are you really fed up?" and I said, "No, I'm not fed up, but I just want to be with horses." He said, "I don't blame you." He told Scotty Cockburn about it and then he said to me, "When you start training horses I want to send you a couple." You could not be much more decent than that, could you? When he did they were the most awful bloody horses!'

By now Neville had another reason for leaving the Army. His life had acquired some purpose. He was courting.

3

It was after Neville had decided to leave the Army that he met Brownie. In view of his total involvement with horses, it was fairly inevitable that he should meet the love of his life at a hunt ball. Twenty-year-old Sylvia Diana Bradley was enough to turn the head of any young man. Blonde, vivacious, with a lovely figure, she had a wonderful sense of humour and was always tremendous fun. 'Brownie was absolutely gorgeous,' says Bruce Hobbs, who was to know her well in a few years' time.

Brownie explains the name which has been hers nearly all her life. 'When I was about three someone gave me an American book about a very naughty little boy called Buster Brown. An aunt started calling me Buster – I even had a Buster suit made, shorts and top. Everybody called me Buster. Then it developed into Brown, which was not very pretty, but then it changed to Brownie and, although the mistresses at school called me Sylvia, which I managed to answer to, my friends have all called me Brownie ever since.

'I was born just outside Birmingham, in Solihull, where my grandmother had a very big house called Tudor Grange. I remember that we had seven gardeners there. My grandfather had been a little chemist in Moseley, a suburb of Birmingham, when they were first married. His name was Alfred Bird.

'My grandmother had a funny tummy and was frightfully bilious. So he invented a custard powder without eggs. That was how Bird's Custard came into being. My grandfather became a millionaire, was knighted and, as Sir Alfred Bird, lived at Tudor Grange. He was always up in London when Parliament was sitting. He had five sons and two daughters. When my mother died my younger sister and I moved into Tudor Grange with my grandmother. My father, who was a

Bradley, made hardware, dustbins, stable buckets and so on. He lived in the Queen's Hotel in Birmingham and used to visit us every week. Then he met my stepmother, married her and bought a house at Shiplake, Henley, in Oxfordshire, because Daddy simply adored boats and had always longed to live by the water. They had two more daughters and when my sister and I went to live with them they had to build an extension onto the house.

'So my poor old grandmother lived all by her self at Tudor Grange and as soon as I got a car at the age of seventeen I used to drive up to stay a few days with her. Both my sister and I were terribly spoilt. There was no need for us to go out of those glorious grounds at Tudor Grange because it was surrounded by lovely fields with sunken fences. It looked just as though you could walk straight into the next field. There were wild duck on the lake. It's a home now, I've never been back.'

Neville was delighted with the way in which Brownie's grandfather, Sir Alfred Bird, had died. He says, "He had always loved the birds. He was in London and saw a smashing girl on the other side of the road, so he ran across and got run over by a bus. He died in Hyde Park Hospital.'

Brownie says, 'He and my grandmother were great cyclists and he had special lightweight bicycles made. They would take them on the train, go to Wales and bicycle back to Solihull. No dropped handlebars, just ordinary upright bikes.

'My grandfather was the first man to have a car in Birmingham. He was so dangerous and frightening that no one would drive with him, except my poor mother who, as a young girl, was always detailed to accompany him. One day they were driving along the road and went round a sharp corner. The chauffeur, who sat up behind with his arms folded like a coachman when the master was driving, suddenly vanished. My grandmother looked back and said, "Where's Bob?" The unfortunate Bob had been thrown out over a hedge into a field and when they went back for him they found he had a broken arm.'

Brownie's involvement with horses started at the age of three, with a Shetland pony called Cossack. 'I had a tiny little governess cart. Cossack was a fairly evil little pony, as nappy as they come. When we came to a crossroads it would rear up and turn the cart over, tipping us out. I used to go driving with the gardener. We had a terrible time. Then I started riding at the local riding school. I never had a horse of my own until Neville gave me a broken-down point-to-pointer. But I did quite a lot of show-jumping successfully. When we got engaged Neville lent me a very nice show-jumping mare called Plenty.

'It's funny the things you remember. I had some very smart, new, red-string gloves, which were most fashionable at the time, and I was very proud of myself. I went to the meet on a chesnut mare, following the Master, Colin McNaughton. We started galloping across a field which looked lovely, lush and green, when suddenly the mare put her foot in a bog and I went head over heels into the mud. When I got up you could not tell whether I was a man or a girl. I was covered in mud from head to foot and had to go home. The red gloves were black!'

Brownie and a friend called Tom Farmiloe were invited to dine at Neville's house before the Hunt Ball. 'When we arrived, there was no Neville. He was riding at Haydock for Sir Arland Freake, who had a small string of horses at Childrey. Neville had two falls and Arland Freake crashed the car coming home, so he was terribly late. When he finally arrived, he said to me, "Oh, you've deigned to come have you!" I thought he was a conceited fool. However, he changed into his evening hunt coat and when we got to the ball he asked me to dance. We stuck together all night long.' They fell in love, announced their engagement and were seldom out of each other's sight.

Brownie travelled with Neville when he went racing. He was delighted to be driven by his fiancée, who was an outstanding driver, so good, in fact that she won the ladies' section of the RAC Rally.

Those were the days when the West Country circuit was at its liveliest and best. When jumping started at the end of July and when the season finished in May and early June, the cavalcade would move down to Torquay, where bookmaker/hotelier, Ben Warner, owned the Queen's Hotel. There were many meetings in that part of the world before the war:

Torquay, Totnes, Buckfastleigh, Newton Abbot, Devon and Exeter were all ideal for moderate National Hunt horses. And they provided a wonderful opportunity for the sporting owners, trainers and jockeys to foregather for one long exciting party by the seaside. As a young man I used to be fascinated by Peter Thrale's stories of these little West Country jumping meetings, particularly Torquay, where on the evenings before the races Ben Warner would entertain the chief trainers in his hotel to go through the programme. 'Gill,' he would say, 'you'd better have the seller. Peter, you haven't won a race for a while, suppose you win the second . . .,' and so on through the card.

One day, while these arrangements were being made, Peter remonstrated, 'But Ben, that's no good. My old horse will be long odds on.' He was told not to worry about that, but to have a good bet at starting price. 'I couldn't believe my eyes,' said Peter later. 'When the animal won it was returned at 3–1 against. It appeared that Ben's control extended to the men who returned the starting price!'

On one such occasion the engaged couple, staying in Ben Warner's hotel, were supposed to be being chaperoned by an owner called Mrs Greenslade. Brownie says, 'One night Neville decided to pay me a visit, got out of the window of his room and fell flat on his back in a flowerbed. He had to walk through the lounge of the hotel in his pyjamas!' Neville says, 'Lucky I had my pyjamas on! All those people sitting there in their evening clothes, and I had to walk through pretending to be nonchalant!

'Some time later, when I left Brownie's room, she said, "You're not going out of my window." I said, "You're right! I'm going downstairs the same way I came!" I shall never forget that. Luckily by then all the people had gone to bed.'

Mrs Greenslade may not have been a very good chaperone, but she had one or two decent horses. Neville recalls, 'The last time I ever rode for her was at Cartmel before the war. I trotted up. But I was also riding in a later race and in those days they had hound trials at the same time. The hound trials took place in the morning and the racing in the afternoon. Unfortunately on this particular occasion an old hound had got himself lost. As I was riding into the last fence, the hound suddenly appeared giving tongue right in front of my horse, who whipped out and put me through the wing, half crucifying me!'

Having left the Army to fulfil his ambition, Neville first had to learn the art of training racehorses. He went straight to the late Sonny Hall, who had seventy horses at Russley Park, near Swindon, one of the most famous training establishments in the land, where the late Atty Persse had trained briefly for Lord Wavertree before moving to Chattis Hill, Stockbridge. If you drive down the M4, going east from Swindon towards London, you will see Russley Park, in the lea of the Downs, as you get towards Lambourn. Like nearly all the great training stables, its very *raison d'être* has proved its undoing in this modern age when stable lads and their families need to be close to a town. In the days when training stables like Russley, Druids Lodge, Foxhill and Chattis Hill were constructed, they were deliberately situated well away from the towns so that their secrets could be guarded. Today, even if you have the best boxes and the finest gallops in the world, you cannot run a racing stable without labour, and modern labour will not work in isolated places. Now these great stables are mostly farms, monuments of days that have gone, never to return.

'Russley was a wonderful place,' Neville says. 'I had to pay Sonny a premium to learn with him.' It was a worthwhile premium. Other pupils included the future royal trainer, Peter Cazalet, Lord Mildmay, who, as the last of the Corinthians, was to be loved and respected by all in racing, and Tom Hanbury, whose son Ben now trains successfully at Newmarket.

Another young cavalry officer who was to become one of Neville's greatest friends was also just about to leave the Army. In 1935 the National had been won by Reynoldstown, trained by his owner Major Noel Furlong, whose son Frank, a 9th Lancers officer, had the ride. Now, in 1936, although the horse was set to carry 12 st 2 lb (12 lb more than the previous year) Frank had such difficulty doing the weight that he offered the mount to his former brother officer, Fulke Walwyn.

It was a sensational National. Mrs Mundy's Avenger, one of the most beautiful quality chasers I have ever seen, was joint favourite with Golden Miller. Anthony Mildmay, then a tall, gangly, inexperienced amateur, was on his own outsider Davy Jones, a tubed, former flat racehorse, trained by Harry Whiteman at Peter Cazalet's home, Fairlawne, in Kent. The Miller fell at the first and, remounted, refused at the ditch after Valentine's. It was Davy Jones who led as they passed the stands for the first time, in front of Avenger, while Fulke was quietly nursing Reynoldstown in the rear. Davy Jones ran out. It was the start of Fairlawne's Aintree disasters which became a hoodoo for the stable in the National ever after. Like the good jockey that he was, Fulke had kept something in hand and now, deprived of opposition, he galloped home twelve lengths clear of Ego, ridden by another Welsh amateur, Harry Llewellyn, who was to thrill the world ten years later with his show-jumping exploits on Foxhunter. Fortified by this success, Fulke Walwyn left the Army to become a professional jockey.

Sonny Hall was a past master at having a tilt at the ring. He loved nothing more than to engineer a starting-price coup. Today bookmakers have a variety of sophisticated devices at their disposal to prevent the gambler from catching them out. Then it was not so difficult. If there was no money for a horse on the racecourse, he would probably be returned at a fairly long price, particularly if the connections were seen to be backing something else. Telegrams were accepted by the bookmakers, provided they were stamped before the off. So the drill was to send people armed with telegram bets round small, country post offices. Provided that this was judiciously done, particularly in fairly small bets, the money never got back to the course in time to affect the starting price.

Neville says, 'Sonny used to have terrific coups. Brownie and I had to go all over the country, sending some telegrams from one post office and some from another. The coups came off very often. He was a cunning old beggar. Moreover he had one or two decent horses and when he was engineering a coup he would probably run the animal down the course one or two times – not that we knew anything about it!'

Neville has never been a betting man. Brownie says, 'I'm the gambler in the family, the only one who bets! I used to love those starting price coups with old Sonny Hall. On bank holidays he had horses everywhere. And the poor old women in the little country post offices never had a chance to get the telegrams through. By the time that they had written it all down the race was over. Marvellous. I wish you could do it now.'

Undoubtedly horses were tougher fifty years ago. There is a difference of opinion as to the reason. Some say that they were a tougher, hardier breed and took more breaking. Others claim that they are much better handled today from the moment that they are foaled. There is probably a certain amount of truth in both claims. Undoubtedly horses had more bone; the old-fashioned steeplechaser was a bigger, more powerful animal than his counterpart today. The late Lord Bicester, keenest of all National Hunt stalwarts and a great judge of jumpers, always insisted on a horse 'who walked as though he had just shat himself'. Those great powerhouse chasers are now no more.

Moreover there were more savage horses in those days. There were two particularly savage four-year-old colts when I was with Atty Persse. Both of them loathed the stable jockey, Michael Beary, who had given them some fairly severe hidings when the money was down. Poor Michael! As we waited in the yard on a Sunday evening we always knew when he was coming round with the Guv'nor. The colts would be the first to hear the high-pitched Irish voice. They would start bellowing and try to climb the walls of the box to get at him.

On the Downs in the morning, when speed was essential, Atty would shout, 'Change Beary onto Nassau. Hurry up, Michael. Jump off.' I would run over to find Michael, white as a sheet, still sitting on the colt he had just ridden a gallop. 'Get a hold of him, Tim,' the great jockey would beg me. 'Are you sure you've got him now? He'll kill me if he gets a chance.' Only when I assured him that I had the colt firmly by the head would Michael slip off and scuttle to his next ride. As long as he was mounted, that wonderful horseman was safe, but once on the ground he knew he was vulnerable.

As soon as a horse left its stable in Berkshire it was automatically working. Training yards were usually built in the valleys between the succession of downland ridges which stretch from East Ilsley right across to Marlborough – those watersheds which have for years boasted the finest natural going in the world, Ogbourne Downs and White Horse Hill, which rise in the triangle between Wantage, Ashbury and Upper Lambourn. There are innumerable hills for horses to trot up steadily, slowly putting on muscle in the right places, building vital condition which should stay with them through the long season ahead. It is the same in Yorkshire where Neville trains today.

On some of those old gallops there were still rubbing houses, little walled enclosures about the size of a big foaling box, where, in the previous century, racehorses would be rubbed down after work. There is one such on Weathercock Hill, that fine old turf gallop above Ashdown House between Upper Lambourn and Ashbury which, in those days, was handy for Russley Park.

Neville says, 'Sonny had a savage horse called Nageesh whom I was going to ride in a bumper race at Aintree. The lad got off and Sonny told me to get on the horse. He created so much that I could not get on, so Sonny said, "Take him in the rubbing-house." As soon as we got him in he reared up, got loose and chased me round and round. I was scuttling like a scared rabbit. I decided I had better run outside, because I would have more of a chance. In the end, as he came out after me, I hit him a good crack on the backside with my whip and he buggered off home. Sonny was furious. "You stupid bastard!" he said. "You'd better come in my car," and he took me back. When we got back to the yard he asked the head lad, "Where's that bloody Nageesh?" "Oh he's in his box." "Who caught him?" "Oh," said the head man, "Old Bert the gardener."

'Of course, the old gardener did not know anything about the horse and, as usually happens with savage horses, was not in the least frightened. He had gone up to him, caught him, whipped his saddle off, clipped him up the backside and let him go in his box. In the end Sonny said, "Well, you're not riding him at bloody Aintree!" To which I replied, "Thank God!" He was a horrible horse.'

Neville's and Brownie's wedding on 11 October 1937, at St George's, Hanover Square, was a party to end all parties for the officers of the 4th Hussars. Brownie says, 'They were all pissed and showed the guests into the wrong pews. Everybody went mad. Stephen Eve, later to become Colonel, was our best man and the night after we left they had a fabulous party in London.

'We decided to spend our honeymoon in the South of France. We drove down in the big old Triumph in which I had won the RAC Rally. As a result the shock absorbers were pretty hard. In those days there were horns on the front of cars, and when we got to Boulogne, driving over the cobbles and bumping about with this hard suspension, the horns fell off. We had to stop and have them wired on. It took us four days to get down to the South of France. It had been such a journey that when we finally got to the Grand Hotel, the bride had to go in to see whether the rooms were in order because Neville could not get out of the car. A little old cripple came along with two sticks, taking one step forward and one step back. I told Neville that was the state he would be in if he did not get out of the car! He was not best pleased.

'We had a wonderful time. When we looked out of the window of our hotel we saw a very fat man being attended by two beautiful girls. That was the late Lord Beaverbrook.'

When they returned after three weeks Neville and Brownie moved into a little cottage belonging to the trainer Bay Powell in the attractive little village of Aldbourne. The cottage had very low beams, like so many old Tudor buildings in that area. Brownie recalls, 'I was riding out one day and Neville was going racing with Sonny, who said he would leave at 11 o'clock whether Neville was ready or not. Neville rushed back to the cottage to change. He forgot about the low beams, charged out of the bedroom, hit his head and knocked himself out for about a quarter of an hour. Sonny went without him!'

The cottage lacked the basic amenities. As Brownie remembers, 'There was no electric light. And no bathroom. We used to go to the pub for a bath.'

Neville chipps in, 'Yes, while the old girl was having a bath I was getting pissed and vice versa! We had a lot of fun there.'

Brownie says, 'I had to take my stockings in my overcoat pocket. It was incredibly cold that winter and there was only an outside lavatory.'

Neville says, 'When we arrived back, after three weeks' honeymoon, Sonny greeted me with "You look a bit weak!" So I said, "Thanks very much. I am!" So he said, "Will you ride Sprightly Archer?" I said, "That's a dirty bloody trick for a start!" So he said, "Right, you'll ride him."

'Now Sprightly Archer was a strong jumper who used to gallop with his head on the ground. Strangely enough, although he would run away with most of the lads, somehow I could manage him. I would say to the lads, "Now, don't go off, keep together and let me sit behind you. Then I'll be all right. Don't open up for Christ's sake, or I'll be gone!"

'This morning Sonny said, "You'll come up half speed." I did not like to argue with him so off we went. We had gone about a hundred yards when the lads opened up and he whooshed off. All Sonny said when I came back was, "I thought I told you to come up half speed. I don't know where the hell you'd find the other half!" He knew I was weak and he was quite right.'

At the end of 1937 Neville took out his first training licence and he and Brownie moved to Upavon on Salisbury Plain in Wiltshire, where they bought a small house and yard.

Neville says, 'I am definitely the oldest licence holder of all the top trainers. Fulke can argue as much as he likes, but I have a picture of him still riding as a professional jockey on Mansur, trained N. Crump.'

Neville started from scratch and in those early days at Upavon he never had more than twelve horses. Nevertheless in the one full season before the war, 1938–39, he trained sixteen winners. The first was Anca, ridden by Sean Magee, at Torquay. Neville says, 'He had won the French Grand National and about twenty races in France before he came to me. A funny little horse, but a bit better class than the rest, even though he was coming to the end of his mileage.

'The best horse I trained before the war was unquestionably Mansur, a grey colt who had finished third in the French Derby and who was bought by Gerald Askew, my old friend from the Surrey and Burstow days, for £300. That's the horse that Fulke is riding in the picture. We did not know much about him. In fact we thought he was a mare. We just had instructions to meet him at Upavon station where he had been sent from Newmarket.'

Brownie continues the story. 'When we opened the railway box there was this enormous grey horse, wearing a hood and three rugs on a blazing hot day. He was covered in sweat. There were no lads about and we hadn't been warned that he was savage, so Neville and I treated him just like any other horse. He came out of the railway truck and just stood looking all around him, taking everything in. We had hired a horsebox to take him back to the yard. But after having been in the train overnight he did not want to go in. We struggled with him and eventually managed to get him back. There we were, Neville and I, crawling about, taking off his knee boots as though he was an old donkey. It just shows that if you are not frightened they never do anything.

'It was only later we learned that he was savage. One day our head lad was exercising him on the road when Mansur gave a huge kick and a buck, firing the lad off. The horse stood over him and didn't savage him – the lad had been knocked out – but when another lad came over to try and get near Mansur savaged the newcomer and his horse. In the end someone in a car got word to Neville who came straight down and sorted it out. We always had trouble boxing him. We had to give him an extra hour because sometimes he would not go in the box. He would just stand there. If you showed him a whip he still would not go in. But he was a hell of a horse. It's a pity he could not go

37

chasing because he would have won some top-class races. He carried the weight. Lovely horse.'

Neville says, 'I had bought from Weedon a really good hunter mare called Shortear, because at some stage of her life she had had the top of one ear bitten off. Her only fault was that she had diseased ovaries, and when you got on her she would buck like hell. My first bad experience of Shortear was when I took her by train to a meet and, all dressed up in my scarlet coat, I got on her and gave her a kick in the ribs to try to catch up with the hunt. That started it. She gave the most enormous buck like a rodeo horse, going back under me and landing me right in a huge heap of coal. Real black coal. At the meet Peter Herbert said, "Are you all right? You ought to see yourself!" I said, "I can't see my back, you old idiot!" So I took my hat off to the Master and carried on.

'But that was by no means the end of Shortear, I got the old troop horse out of the Army and she was magnificent at leading the young jumpers.'

Brownie recalls the day when Gerald Askew came to stay at Upavon and Neville asked him whether he would like to ride out. When he said 'Yes', Neville told him that he could ride Shortear. Neville himself was riding a racehorse. Brownie continues, 'There was a wall running down one side of the yard. I just happened to be coming out of the front door when Gerald was mounting. Suddenly I heard a terrible commotion and Gerald shouting, "Oh, oh, oh, oh!" All I could see was Gerald's body going up and down above the wall. Shortear was bucking like hell, as she always did. It was not a very comfortable introduction for the owner of our best horse!'

Neville says, 'Fulke was going to ride Mansur at Ludlow. So we asked him down to ride the horse at school. I had nothing to school with him except Shortear. Mansur was a stallion and Fulke was not at all happy when he found he was going to school with a little common mare. I said, "Go on! You can follow her." He said, "Don't be bloody ridiculous. I'll be up her backside! This horse will be covering her!"

'So off we went. Fulke was purple in the face. I set off and went like hell over the hurdles and Fulke came past me shouting, "You bloody idiot!" I said, "Well, at least he can jump. That's all we wanted to find out."'

Neville won some good races with Mansur. He even won the Gloucester Hurdle at Cheltenham's National Hunt Festival in his first season.

Fulke had not long been married to the former Diana Carlos-Clarke. Di was not only the most beautiful woman that most of us had ever seen, but she was also a brilliant horsewoman, schooling or riding work. Bruce Hobbs recalled the day, soon after the war, when Di was riding fast work on a nasty hard-pulling horse, whose girth snapped after a furlong. 'Of course, the saddle went,' said Bruce, 'but far from panicking, she went the full mile and a quarter, never looked like falling off and pulled up as though nothing had happened. She was brilliant.'

Brownie says, 'Fulke rode his very last winner on Mansur. We were in an early race on that fateful day at Ludlow in 1939, and after we had won Neville and I set off for home, so we missed Fulke's terrible crash, when he cracked his skull. Di probably shouldn't have done it but she rattled Fulke all the way back to the Nuffield Hospital in Oxford in their car. My father-in-law was very friendly with Lord Nuffield and Neville was able to pull a few strings to make sure that Fulke got the best attention, but for a very long time he could not speak. He had lost his speech and was terribly slow, so that it was a job to understand what he was saying. He was extremely lucky not to have been killed.'

When he recovered, Fulke started on that wonderful career as a trainer which has so delighted his old friend Neville. The first winner ever 'trained F. T. Walwyn' was ridden by Trooper Bruce Hobbs of the North Somerset Yeomanry.

As soon as they moved to Upavon Neville, realizing sooner than most that war was inevitable, joined the North Somerset Yeomanry. The first person he met was the regimental sergeant major – none other than his old friend from the 4th Hussars, Dickie Bird, who was absolutely delighted to see him. 'Come on, sir!' he said. 'We'll smarten some of these fellows up all right!'

Neville was twenty-eight. He knew war was coming. Here, as his biographer, I find the first insight into the intense loyalty which was to characterize the man throughout his life. For his wife, the lovely, witty, sparkling Brownie, he had already developed an intense love which was to stay with him to the exclusion of all others throughout his life. For those who worked for him, like Dickie Bird, he was to stand up with that unique form of unswerving loyalty which belongs to the British services and has made our country great. Moreover, working his horses on those lovely downland gallops, Neville was already demonstrating the attention to detail, love of the individual animal and complete involvement with his men and horses that never left him.

I suppose everyone knew that war was inevitable but, with fervent wishful thinking, they made themselves believe that it would never happen. There was Munich and Chamberlain with his little bit of paper and 'Peace in our time'. One of Sir Gordon Richards's favourite sayings is 'Once a Downsman, always a Downsman'. For Neville and Brownie in their little paradise at Upavon, however, the preparations for war on Salisbury Plain were all too obvious. Nevertheless the racing circus went on.

One day, when they were riding back from the Downs, Neville saw smoke rising from what he thought was their cottage. He started to gallop off towards it, only to be stopped by the head lad who said, 'We'd better not make the horses sweat, sir.' So they went on walking down. As luck would have it, it was not their house at all but the one next door, lived in by David Dawnay, later to be General Sir David Dawnay, Clerk of the Course at Ascot.

Brownie laughs. 'I'll tell you about another officer,' she says. 'We won a good race at Fontwell and were given a case of champagne for the owner. We put it in the back of the car, but we were not going back to Upavon. Not immediately that is. We were off for the Western Circuit where we had runners over the weekend, staying, as usual at Torquay. You could run a horse on the Saturday and again on the Monday.

'When we got back home we were met by the winning

owner, who said, "What about my champagne?" Neville said, "I'm sorry, but it's all gone!" I am afraid that, sure enough, the case was empty. The owner was furious. You'd have thought that he would have been only too pleased. After all, he'd won the race at Fontwell and had all the glory. You'd have thought he would have liked his trainer to be able to celebrate!'

Brownie gives one of her irrepressible giggles. 'What's the matter?' says Neville. 'I was thinking of the time your father made you row miles on the river,' said his wife. 'This was quite a while before we were married. Mother was taken short in the night and caught Neville coming out of my room at 3 o'clock in the morning. We were going to be dispatched to India. Why India I can't think. Imagine! Just because we slept together!'

The little racing circus had drifted down to the West Country as usual at the end of July of that last uneasy summer in the aftermath of Munich. It was obvious that the writing was on the wall, and the declaration of war in September produced the inevitable recall to the colours of Captain Neville Crump, now of the North Somerset Yeomanry.

The halcyon days were over for Neville and Brownie. From their little Upavon home they had to disperse their small string and, within a very short time, Neville had to report to Weston-super-Mare where the regiment was being assembled. There, in addition to the drill and the basic training, the North Somerset Yeomanry, a motley collection of butchers, bakers and candlestickmakers, were preparing to receive their horses. In retrospect it is easy to ridicule the overall strategy of 1939, when England was hardly ready for war. We were pitifully short of aircraft, tanks, anti-tank weapons, every sort of vehicle, armoured and otherwise – all the paraphernalia needed to oppose the Wehrmacht.

Despite twenty-one years of peace, memories still persisted of the German threat to the vital Middle East through the Balkans and Turkey. Britain and her far-flung Empire, standing alone against the might of Nazi Germany, needed at least a presence in this area to thwart the threat and there were still men in high places who had served with Allenby. So it was decided to send out to Palestine, as it then was, a Yeomanry

Division, fully equipped as horse cavalry with 6000 horses and men.

We should give someone in the higher command the credit for appreciating that, although the horses would never be used in anger, at least top-quality, trained men would be on the spot, ready for speedy mechanization when the necessary equipment became available. After all, the Ordnance stores were still bursting with cavalry equipment, turned in after 1918 as regiment after regiment had been mechanized. Of the regulars only the Household Cavalry, the Royal Dragoons and the Royal Scots Greys had retained their horses. The last two famous regiments had already been in Palestine for a year, policing the country and keeping the peace between Arabs and Jews with considerable success. So they were now to be joined by a fully horsed Yeomanry Division.

At Weston-super-Mare the North Somerset Yeomanry made preparations to receive their horses, who were to be picketed on the rugby football ground. While civilians, now equipped with gas masks, were filling sandbags, digging trenches, erecting air-raid shelters and building beach fortifications, the Yeomanry were establishing forage centres, putting up water troughs and digging in posts to which to tie the strong ropes, 3–4 feet high, that formed the breast lines for tethering their horses. Among the new soldiers from every walk of life there were quite a few fairly reasonable horsemen, including the occasional exceptional one, like the tall eighteen-year-old, Trooper Bruce Hobbs, who had ridden Battleship to victory in the previous year's Grand National, the youngest and tallest jockey on the smallest horse to triumph in the world's greatest steeplechase.

Bruce, whose life story, *No Secret So Close*, I was privileged to write, and who is now a member of the Jockey Club after completing a highly successful training career, recalls, 'The day came when we had to go and find all our horses. It was great fun for me because, since there were very few who knew anything about horses at all, I was on every single horse party. We went all over Cornwall on trains, rounding up horses. They had been commandeered in advance. Sixty pounds was the top price the Army was paying for a horse. We had to go down and collect them at the addresses which we had been given. There were all sorts – thoroughbreds, show horses, well-bred hunters, hairy-legged cobs.

'Having assembled them, we had to load them into cattle trucks, nose to tail, eight to a truck, packed in so tight that they couldn't kick each other. As they were on permanent standing lines, each horse had one heel shackled to a heel line on the ground to prevent him from kicking his neighbour. Horses were fed in nosebags and each animal had a haynet attached to the rope in front of him. For watering, one man would normally lead four horses at a time to the trough. Picket guards were posted to look after the horses day and night. We already had our rifles and now came the great moment when every man was issued a saddle, bridle and full equipment for a cavalryman. Then everyone was given a horse. Needless to say, as I had selected and collected them, I picked a particularly good sort for myself!'

A few years earlier, in the 4th Hussars, Neville had been in charge of the riding school. He did a great job and, as I was to discover myself a little later, he was an outstanding instructor. Even at this stage of his career it was obvious that he was meticulous and completely dedicated to horses and the way in which they were ridden and looked after. No detail was spared, nothing was too much trouble. It has been the same ever since. Now, in the North Somerset Yeomanry, he had a formidable task. In a short time he had to teach both riders and horses. Most of the horses were very moderately trained and at least five hundred of the riders had never been on anything other than a pony on the sands, if that!

When a cavalry horse appeared on parade, the rider's sword was already strapped to the saddle behind the flap on the near or left side of the animal. On the right, or off, side in the same position was the rifle bucket, a long polished leather container in which the trooper's rifle was carried.

The Lee Enfield .303 rifle, designed to stand the stress of all active-service conditions, was large, long, heavy and cumbersome. It was hard enough to teach mounting and dismounting with the rifle to regular recruits, with well-trained steady old troop horses in an indoor school, but Neville and his Yeomanry instructors were faced with the task of teaching raw civilians to perform the same exercise with ordinary, part-trained horses on the grass, in the open, whipped by the sea breeze at Weston-super-Mare.

Bruce recalls, 'When we had our first squadron parade, all four troops lined up and the Squadron Leader ordered mount. It was the funniest sight I have ever seen – sheer pandemonium! There were horses up trees, up lamp-posts, in the gardens of seaside villas, galloping back through the streets to the rugby pitch with everything flapping . . . Soldiers falling off, or hopping round with one foot in the stirrup, trying to get their rifles into the right position, hitting their horses over the head, on the flanks, everywhere . . . Talk about the Crazy Gang! Even they were never so good!'

And Neville recalls, 'We used to train on the sands at Weston. One day Dickie Bird and I were trying to cope with a large squad of these wretched chaps, who knew absolutely nothing and had no idea. One of them suddenly went spare. The old horse took complete charge and hurtled past us quite out of control. The recruit's hat was on the back of his head, his chinstrap was under his nose, and he was lying back on the horse's quarters. It was a marvellous sight. As he went past Dickie Bird shouted, "Goodbye. Send us a postcard when you get there!" I said, "You rotten old sod!" He said, "He'll be all right. He can put the horse into the sea when he gets to the other end. He'll be all right!" Dickie Bird is about eighty now. He always sends us a Christmas card with a little bird on it.'

The North Somerset Yeomanry progressed until it was time for the Yeomanry Division, strengthened now by the Household Cavalry – the Life Guards and Royal Horse Guards (the Blues) – to assemble in the Dukeries. In addition to being in charge of the riding school, Lieutenant Neville Crump was now a troop leader in A Squadron. The regiment moved up to Ollerton, where the officers' mess was in the Hop Pole Hotel. Neville's troop was billeted in the village hall, just by the railway line, and their horses in various farm buildings.

Bruce recalls, 'As my troop leader, knowing that I had spent my life with horses, Neville appointed me as feeder and clipper. At first we had a hand machine to clip the horses with. As you can well imagine, the blades got blunt and the chain was always breaking. From that we graduated to a more sophisticated clipping machine which worked off the battery of a motorcar. When I told him that, feeding thirty-two horses and keeping them all clipped, I had too much to do, he said, "In that case you had better be my Second Servant." There were usually two horses for the officer and one for his servant, but as long as the regiment was in England the odd hunter was apt to be added. Naturally, horses and tack had to be perfectly turned out at all times. For this job I received the princely sum of five shillings extra a week. That was all right for a while, but eventually I got bored with Neville returning from hunting with filthy horses at 5 o'clock on a Saturday evening. So I went back to feeding, about which I had learned so much all my life from my father and his head man.'

The training at Ollerton was fairly basic. Apart from rifle firing on the range, the Yeomanry did very little troop training. No manoeuvres with the horses. Foot drill and mounted drill. More sword drill, by now graduating to mounted dummy-thrusting, that is, charging straw-filled dummies in different positions, representing the bodies of the enemy. The instructors have always held that a straw-filled dummy is much tougher to pierce than flesh and blood. 'Your sword will go into a man like a knife through butter!' they would say gruesomely. How they knew this I have not the slightest idea. They had certainly never used their swords in anger!

The dummy course could be quite hair-raising. In the advanced stages, as you jumped a fence a dummy would come at your head, and you had to parry with the hilt of your sword. Suddenly there would be another dummy on the ground with which you would have to deal. It made you very dextrous and certainly helped to strengthen your seat.

Brownie came up to Ollerton. Christmas passed and then in January 1940 the Yeomanry Division got ready to move to the Middle East. Officially, of course, they were not supposed to know where they were going, but as they had to draw tropical equipment, it was fairly obvious that they were not going to Norway.

It was heart-breaking for Neville to have to leave behind his bride of only two years at Upavon. Brownie says, 'There was a marvellous old character called Howard Alexander who lived in the village. He was a gentleman farmer who wore a grey bowler hat and nearly drank himself into the grave. I went to work for him, milking cows. I had never milked a cow in my life, but I learned. I ended up top girl, the head dairymaid!

'One day I set the dairy on fire, trying to light the boiler for the steam. I put paraffin on it and whoof! up it went. The cottage was thatched and luckily the other girl who was working with me and I just managed to put it out in time, with buckets of water. Old Howard Alexander never said a word, because I was a good worker and he was frightened I might leave. I was paid ninepence a day!'

The Fourth Brigade of the 1st Cavalry Division included the North Somerset Yeomanry and the Household Cavalry. They had travelled up from Somerset by train and now had to be organized for the big move to the South Coast for embarkation. They were sorted into those who were going to be in charge of the horses and those who were going by troop ship. Naturally Neville and Bruce were chosen for the horse party and their vet was Frank Cundell, a wonderful man, who was later to become one of the most successful and outstandingly popular jumping trainers. When he died he was mourned by the entire racing world. Lieutenant Crump, of course, had his charger. The soldiers, including Trooper Hobbs, riding one and leading two, with no saddles, just ordinary jute rugs on the horses, went from Ollerton to Tuxford to entrain for Dover.

This time there were no luxury trucks, just cattle wagons, eight horses to each truck, watering at stations en route, stopping occasionally because a horse had kicked out the side of a cattle waggon, rattling through snow-covered fields in that cold January. It was a hard winter as a nation prepared belatedly for war, with every different kind of uniform to be seen, tin hats, gas masks, women in uniform, blackout and the

46

onset of austerity. Total war was about to shake our civilization and revolutionize our way of life. The Yeomany did not realize that they were an anachronism as England struggled to mechanize. They firmly believed that they were going to war with their 6000 horses. On arrival at Dover they somehow succeeded in embarking them all onto channel steamers and down into the holds. It was one of the most extraordinary operations ever known in war or peace.

Bruce recalls, 'It was a hell of a job, I was tremendously excited and I remember our boat steering round a mine while we fired our rifles at it. Perhaps fortunately, it did not explode. When we got to Dunkirk there was a scene of complete chaos, because all these horses were arriving and they had to be loaded with no proper ramps into enormous metal wagons with two double doors in the middle. We had to put eight horses into each wagon, four on each side facing inwards, tethered to a rope, with four men in the gangway between them. The loading went on all night long, under floodlights. It was ghastly because, although our horses were well shod, there was no straw and the floors of the wagons were absolutely smooth. Our manpower consisted not only of inexperienced yeomen, but French dockers and assorted helpers who knew nothing whatsoever about horses. Slapping, pulling, pushing, encouraging, we somehow got all the animals onto the train and set off on the four-day journey down to Marseilles.'

The advance party had done its job well. There were army kitchens and forage stores at various halts along the way where the train stopped for the English soldiers to water and feed their horses and themselves. 'We were able to mix feeds in their individual nosebags for the horses, but we ourselves had only haversack meals – not a hot meal on the four days' trip.'

They finally arrived at a little halt just outside Marseilles called appropriately Château Renard. 'It was an enormous castle and there were horses everywhere,' says Bruce. 'The weather was exceptionally treacherous. It was lovely and warm when we arrived but it had been so wet beforehand that the horse lines were flooded. We ourselves were sleeping in bell tents, but the duckboards were, for the most part, floating.

Our horses were once again on breast lines, but on the second night the weather changed and it froze so hard that I saw four big black Household Cavalry horses standing stark and stiff, frozen to death on the lines.

'We stayed at Château Renard for four nights and then were on the move again, riding and leading into Marseilles. As soon as I saw those cobbled streets, I dismounted quickly and so advised the others around me. But I was only a trooper and was in no position to give orders. So, as they had not been warned in advance, many of the party did not appreciate the danger, and horses were going down like ninepins. A number cut their knees badly. When we arrived at the docks we loaded the horses onto a boat which had previously carried mules. They had to go right down into the hold. There were wings on either side of the gangway and the only way to get the horses on was to let them loose, aim them at the opening, crack a whip behind them and say, "Go on!" There was somebody at the other end to tether them up. The pens were built for mules, so, although they were fitted in fairly tightly, each horse had its own little partition. There were horses from the hold right up to the top deck, as many as three hundred to a boat.

'We had all our saddlery, personal equipment and kit – sacks and sacks of it – on board. I had my racing breeches, boots, whip and goodness knows what else strapped to the underside of my saddle, on the old army principle that "A good soldier is never parted from his kit". Neville Crump and Frank Cundell were on our boat. We slept in hammocks on the horse deck, more cramped than the animals in fact. The crew were Lascars and it was quite interesting, in a gruesome sort of way, to watch them making the bread, kneading it with their feet and spitting on it. However, we never got any tummy bugs, but two horses died.

'During the five-day voyage poor Frank Cundell and his veterinary assistants worked flat out the whole way, chiefly because of the Household Cavalry horses, many of whom were so soft from living indoors all the time that they were constantly sick with colic and every other sort of illness. One mare gave birth to a foal.

'We had to wait until dark until we could manhandle the two dead horses into slings, slit their bellies open to make them sink and let the cranes put them overboard. It was vital that enemy submarines should not find the trail of blood. As we had set out, Lord Haw-Haw announced on the radio that the Fourth Brigade of the 1st Cavalry Division were setting sail from Marseilles and would be the first convoy success for the Führer.'

Nevertheless at this stage most of the German war effort was concentrated on the impending invasion of the Low Countries and France, with the result that the North Somerset Yeomanry's voyage through the Mediterranean was without incident and they arrived safely at Haifa five days after leaving Marseilles. The regiment had been brought up to fighting strength by the addition of a number of reservists from regular cavalry regiments, some of whom were old sweats, but others, excellent men by any standards, were to prove a tremendous asset. Bruce had become friendly with several of these men, including 'a cracking chap' called Dusty Dewster, and began to learn some of the ways and means of army life.

The saddlery issued to the Yeomanry was, for the most part, unused and contained bits and stirrup irons made of steel, which had to be burnished to keep clean. No such chore was required of the Household Cavalry troopers because all their bits and irons had been chromium-plated.

'It seemed unfair,' says Bruce, 'that they should have the best tack. Four of us decided that something would be done about it and, somehow or other, by the time we came to disembark, our troop was fully equipped with chrome bits and irons. Nothing dishonest. Nothing stolen. Just a few members of the Blues having to work a little harder than usual – like the rest of us!'

Neville said, 'I don't remember much about that journey, except that it was bloody hard work for Frank and me because, I suppose, we knew more about horses than anyone else on the ship. Frank got very drunk one night. He had spent a lot of his life in India, where he won the Indian Grand National a couple of times. The commanding officer, a rather grand fellow from the Household Cavalry, was somewhere else on the ship when Frank decided to show all those smart young officers how the Indians wipe their bottoms. To everyone's delight he got a saucer and some water, took down his trousers and was showing them, when in walked the commanding officer. "Cundell," he said, "what are you doing?" "I suppose you think I'm teaching your officers bad manners," said Frank. "Actually, Colonel, I'm teaching them good manners if ever they go to India!"'

After the austerity of wartime England and the blackout at home and on the ship, Palestine seemed like another planet, particularly to nineteen-year-old Bruce, whose only venture abroad had been a heavily escorted trip to the United States nearly two years earlier, following his Grand National triumph on the American stallion Battleship.* Haifa in those days, although capable of taking ships of fairly considerable draught, was more like a seaside resort than a port, perhaps a modernized Mediterranean version of Deauville Trouville. The bright lights shone at night, the shops were full, good food and drink abounded, the girls were pretty and childhood biblical concepts of Mount Carmel were shattered by the discovery that there were nightclubs at the top and bottom and brothels halfway up! Outside the towns many parts of the Holy Land in early spring were sheer joy, with the citrus groves, terraced olive trees and, in the hills, the most glorious wild flowers in the world. 'Haifa was a revelation,' says Neville. 'It was like a holiday town.'

The North Somerset Yeomanry assembled and reorganized at Hadera, a short way from Haifa. After a few weeks they moved as a regiment to the permanent barracks at Jenin. 'It was only half a day's march, but we did it as our first regimental exercise, with leading section, leading troop, squadron, flank guards and so on.'

There is no doubt that modern cavalry tactics of caution allied to dash, when adapted later to mechanized warfare,

---

* The following account is based on my life of Bruce Hobbs, *No Secret So Close* (Pelham Books, 1984).

were responsible for considerable success and lack of casualties in those formations which had been trained in their use. With the notable exceptions of the Greys, the Royals and the Household Cavalry, many of the other cavalry regiments which had been mechanized for some time before the war suffered badly because they believed that dash was the chief characteristic of a cavalryman, even when it was patently foolhardy. They had never experienced the naked feeling of the leading section and troop of a horsed cavalry squadron and regiment on longer bounds. So they moved like a caterpillar, covered at every stage and ready to deploy immediately into attack or defence at the first sign of danger. This conception of tactics was to pay handsome dividends and save many lives in the years to come.

Moreover horse-training produces the finest NCOs imaginable. They have to develop an eye for the country. On an ordinary routine march the leading squadron leader had to be as good a judge of pace as the best flat-race jockey. The march table worked out at exactly 6 miles in the hour, provided that you stuck to the rules. Trot fifteen minutes, walk ten, trot fifteen, dismount and walk ten, halt ten, in each hour.

Many of today's trainers do not realize that, whatever the pace the leading horse is going in front of a long string or column, those in the rear will be going twice as fast trying to catch up. So it is essential when trotting, for instance, that the leader go no faster than a slow hound jog, otherwise those behind will be cantering in order to keep up. Similarly a lot of nonsense is talked about horses being made to walk out. This is the greatest possible mistake. Animals quickly lose condition from walking and trotting too fast. Neville had, from an early age, learned this lesson, and it was to stand him in good stead later on.

After a pre-arranged halt for lunch, with refreshment for horse and man, the regiment would be on its way again, arriving at the appointed place at exactly the anticipated time. There the advanced party, who had left in vehicles the same morning, would have selected the site for the night, erected horse lines and made all necessary arrangements. The squadron sergeant major was normally in charge of the advance party.

An officer's first duty was to see that his animals were correctly groomed, watered, fed and secured, fore and aft, for the night. Then he had to make sure that his soldiers were equally well cared for. The food would already have been prepared and would be waiting for them. Then he could see to himself, and if his first servant was any good, he would find himself well organized.

In March 1940, when Captain Crump, Trooper Hobbs and the North Somerset Yeomanry arrived at Jenin, they were fortunate to find a fully equipped, permanent camp with hutted accommodation for the men and well-drained lines on a concrete base for the horses. Jenin was an ideally situated station, close to Haifa and within easy distance of both Jerusalem and Rehovoth, lying in the plain with the hills as an attractive backdrop to the east. Now the regiment was able to get down to some serious training and, for the first time, to adopt a normal army routine. The yeoman were issued with tropical kits, KD (khaki drill), lightweight breeches, shirts and tunics, with solar topees. Riding, exercising and drilling, they looked supremely fit as, stripped to the waist and all as brown as berries, they strapped their horses on the open-air lines at evening stables.

Bruce was still troop feeder and was horrified to find that, instead of oats, the stable diet was barley, which was always considered to be very blood-heating, tiffin, a kind of chopped-straw chaff, and a particularly rich hay called *dreis*, which was almost entirely sainfoin or lucerne. He need not have worried. For many years the British cavalry had been accustomed to feeding their horses in hot climates and he discovered that the heat counteracted any bad effects that the rich forage might have had.

With Captain Neville Crump as the officer in charge of the riding school, the recruits quickly became capable horsemen. To an outsider it was obvious that tall, impeccably turned-out, highly efficient Bruce would not remain a trooper for much longer. Even the social aspect was becoming a trifle embarrassing. He says, 'Officers and men were not allowed to mix socially. For instance, while we were at Ollerton, if we wanted to go to the Hop Pole pub at night, any officers who were there would reluctantly have to tell us to depart. But very soon, by arrangement, we had a little corner of the dining room curtained off so that we, as other ranks, could go and have a little nosh as well!

'One night, while we were stationed at Jenin, Neville Crump, Frank Cundell and Hector Gordon decided to go to Tel Aviv for a night on the tiles. They had to have an armed escort and asked me to go with them. However, as armed escort, I was lumbered with a rifle and a bandolier containing ninety rounds of ammunition. "That's all right," said Neville. "Give it to the barman!" That's exactly what I did.'

By May a cavalry OCTU (Officer Cadet Training Unit) had been formed at Karkur and Bruce with two other yeomen, Noel Palmer and Tony Dufosee of the famous Wiltshire hunting-chasing farming family, were selected to do the six-month course which should make them into officers. Bruce's selection was opposed by his squadron leader, Major Jimmy Spence, and second in command Hector Gordon, on account of his age – he was still only nineteen – but they were overruled by his commanding officer.

'There were nineteen of us on the course, including my old friend Bill Payne from the Staffordshire Yeomanry and Tom Pettifer from the Warwickshires. I have never enjoyed six months in my life as much as I enjoyed that. We worked hard, played hard and generally had the greatest fun. It was at Karkur that the foundations were laid of a friendship between Bill, Tom and myself which was to last for the remainder of our lives.'

Bill Payne, at the age of seventeen, had been unlucky not to win the Grand National on Great Span. Son of an excellent trainer for whom Bruce had often ridden, Bill was so tough that he had nearly become a professional boxer instead of a jockey. All three enjoyed life to the full but perhaps Tom was the most mischievous.

The commandant and chief instructor at Karkur, which

became known as the Middle East Cavalry School, was Major 'Doodle' Stanton, an enormous man, one of half a dozen officers of 6 feet 4 inches or over in the Greys at that time. The equitation officer was also a Grey, Major 'Tubby' Martyr, assisted by Sergeant Major Fountain from the KDGs and Sergeant Whalley from the Greys. Ferris St George and Peter Herbert came from the Household Cavalry. Neville Crump soon found his way to Karkur with Frank Cundell accompanying him as veterinary officer.

Concurrently the Middle East Cavalry School ran a course for officers which I was lucky enough to attend while Bruce was at the OCTU, and so I can appreciate the excellence of the training he received. 'I learned every branch of horsemanship and horsemastership,' he says. 'For the first two months we never put a saddle on our horses but rode them in just blankets and surcingles. This taught us balance in the most amazing way. As a lifetime professional I could do plenty of things to and with a horse, but now I learned to shoe, rasp and extract teeth, deal with all minor ailments, groom, trim, feed and subject the horse to every form of indignity, such as giving it a physic ball, washing out its sheath and, when necessary, backraking it. Tactics, bookwork, arms drill, every sort of training in the classroom and in the field. Into those six months, Doodle Stanton, an officer of extraordinary intelligence, and his instructors condensed the entire eighteen-month course from the famous Cavalry School at Weedon plus so much more that was required to turn young recruits into capable officers, fit for the war that was already upon us.'

I can personally vouch for the fact that Neville played a great part in the tuition and that his inspired instruction helped Bruce, Bill Payne and Tom Pettifer to be commissioned in the regiment of their choice, the Yorkshire Dragoons. It was a fabulous course. We worked hard and played hard, and we were very young and fit. There was hunting with the Ramleh Vale Foxhounds, racing, shooting and, in the evening, drinking and 'birding', usually in Tel Aviv.

When my regiment, the Greys, was stationed at nearby Rehovoth, the most attractive girls were to be found in the

54

Yemenite quarters, which was strictly out of bounds to all ranks. Imagine the surprise of one of my brother officers when, driving past this part of the town one morning, he saw two grey horses which he suddenly recognized as his own chargers tied up outside one of the little houses. Rupert Milburn was surprised, but nothing like as much as his second servant when his officer burst in and discovered him in the arms of a Yemenite girl!

When Bruce, Bill and Tom joined as second lieutenants, the Yorkshire Dragoons were stationed at Acre, another well-built permanent cavalry camp on the coast near Haifa. Bruce says, 'We were billeted right next door to the Colonel and before dinner on our first night we were introduced all round. Everyone was smartly dressed and we were very well received from the start. At dinner Bill Payne, the senior of our threesome, was put on the Colonel's right; I was on the Colonel's left and Tom was opposite. In the middle of dinner the Mess Sergeant told me that I was wanted on the telephone by Captain Crump. Covered in confusion, I excused myself and went to the telephone to find Neville offering rides for all three of us for the next day's meeting at Sarafand. "Two winners for you, me boy!" he said. I told him that it was extremely awkward because we had only just joined the regiment and that I would ring him back a bit later.

'During dinner the conversation turned to racing and I muttered something to the Colonel about the meeting the next day. "Oh yes, I heard about that, Hobbs," said Colonel Stephenson. I gulped. "That telephone call was from Captain Neville Crump," I said. "He trains horses back home and I was with him in the North Somerset Yeomanry and he's asked me if I could go as he has a couple of rides for me and a ride for Pettifer." I was bright red and sweating with embarrassment. The Colonel laughed. "Of course you can go!" he said. "We'll all come and have a bet!"

'So off we all went the next day to Sarafand, where I rode a double and Bill rode a winner. From that moment we were in. Thereafter we started having races of our own on the sands at Acre – 3½ furlong scurries, which were good for a bet. Then we had regimental sports, athletics, boxing, riding, show-jumping competitions. One of our more dangerous pastimes was keeping the verminous jackal population down by galloping across the plain after them, carrying polo sticks with the heads removed and a piece of lead put on the end. It was the greatest of fun, but because of the cracks in that awful cotton soil there were one or two frightful falls.'

Rabies was, and probably still is, rife in the Middle East. Neville recalls, 'One day Mouse Townsend asked me, "Have you ever seen a rabid man?" I told him that I hadn't and he said I had better come and have a look. He took me to a big sort of tower and instructed me to look through a slit, where I saw a man sitting in a corner. All of a sudden he leaped up and screamed at the walls, waving his hands. "I can't watch this!" I said. Then he did it again. He followed this by taking off his trousers, hurling them around the room and then putting them over the top of his head. I felt physically sick, so I asked Mouse why I had to see this. He said he thought it would do me good, just to see someone who was dying of rabies. When we hunted those jackals afterwards with polo sticks loaded with lead, I whacked them over the head doubly hard.

'Poor old Frank, silly sod, went out in a pair of jodhpurs one day. A jackal jumped up and bit him. He had to have a course of twelve incredibly painful injections in his stomach.'

Neville has never been without a dog. Inevitably he had one in the Middle East. 'Super bitch with a short tail,' he says. 'But she had puppies and she took them down a bloody great well and we couldn't get them out. We had a hell of a job. We managed it in the end but what a performance!'

Soon after he arrived in the Middle East about a hundred Poles came over into Palestine from Syria, wanting to join the British Army. 'They were a real tough lot,' said Neville, 'and I was appointed to look after them. I got on very well with them all, particularly a man who was to become very famous later, General Sikorsky. One evening there was a big Polish Roman Catholic church festival. They had all been drinking gallons of Palestinian vodka, and Hector Gordon, Frank and I went off to church with them. We returned in our old car and at the gate

Neville's mother

A youthful Neville at
Marlborough in 1925

Rectory Farm – Neville's childhood home

The Balliol eight at Henley in 1930. Neville is at number two

Neville being led in after winning at Aldershot in 1933

Point-to-pointing in the thirties – Neville is in the centre

Sandown Park in the early thirties –
amateur rider Neville is in the lead (white
sleeves and cap)

Right: At Upavon in 1938

Neville leading in one of his very first winners as a trainer. 'Loopy', now Colonel Sir L. G. Kennard BT, is on the right in a bowler hat

Mansur, trainer N. Crump, ridden F. Walwyn, 1939. The picture which proves that Neville, not Fulke, is the longest serving licensed trainer!

Mansur, (ridden by F. Walwyn)
7 yrs by Mandar — Senora II
Winner of Clarence Hurdle, Windsor; Gloucestershire Hurdle, Cheltenham; Derbyshire Hurdle, Uttoxeter 1939

In Palestine in 1940

Brownie at Newcastle races just after the war

Captain Neville Crump on another sort of mount at Barnard Castle

The Grand National in 1948. In the winner's enclosure after the race are Sheila's Cottage, Neville and the owner, Mr J. Proctor

Teal ridden by Arthur Thompson -- another National winner for Neville

Sporting Link in action, with Arthur Thompson in the saddle

'A splendid chaser' – Mrs Bache Hay's Goosander with Arthur Thompson up

the sentry said, "Halt!". We couldn't stop. We put the brake on and it didn't work because we were going so fast. We hit the gate and went on through. We lived to tell the story!'

By this time the cavalry regiments were in the process of getting mechanized. It was to be the end of the road for the Yeomanry Division in the role which they imagined they had been sent out to play. As the late Field Marshall Lord Ironside, Chief of the Imperial General Staff, reveals in his diary,* he was, in his own words, 'flabbergasted' when he first came to the War Office at the appalling deficiences in the equipment of the Army and at the very long time that it would take to make them good. There were not enough battle tanks for our one and only Armoured Division when the war started and only two battalions of army tanks for the Infantry Division. So, realizing a need for a presence in the Middle East, however unsuitable it might be for repelling a genuine German drive down towards the Suez Canal and the Gulf, he surreptitiously started building up the troops in the Middle East and also, as he put it, 'sneaked out' the Mounted Division to Palestine.

As armoured fighting vehicles eventually managed to filter through to the Middle East, it was possible to mechanize and equip first the Royals, then the Greys, followed by the Household Cavalry and the Yeomanry regiments, of which the Yorkshire Dragoons, with Colonel Simon Lycett-Green and Bruce Hobbs, was one. The Cheshire Yeomanry and the North Somerset Yeomanry were not so fortunate. They were made into line-of-communication signallers and virtually disbanded as a regiment.

So the former regular officer, Captain Neville Crump, was posted back to England. 'It took months to get home. We travelled back on a new luxury cruise ship, the *Andes*. My travelling companions included Ian Collins, the tennis player, and Peter Fitzwilliam, the Earl of Fitzwilliam, who owned and bred some good racehorses on the flat and was later to be killed in an aircrash. We had to go round the Cape because the Mediterranean was no longer considered safe after Italy's

---

* *The Ironside Diaries 1937–1940* (Constable, 1962).

entry into the war. It was rough going. Then we had to go to Canada, to Port Halifax in Nova Scotia, to pick up some Canadian troops. We stayed in Canada for about a month. It must have taken us nearly three months, before we got back to England (in 1941).'

4

As soon as he returned to England Neville was put in charge of tank training with the 61st Training Regiment at Barnard Castle on the borders of Durham and North Yorkshire, in normal times a wonderful sporting county. There, by the historic town where Charles Dickens wrote Nicholas Nickleby and where Sir Walter Scott was inspired to write Rokeby, Neville and Brownie were reunited. Their love flowered again and on the 9 July 1942 their daughter Sarah was born. They shared a little house in a village close to the town with several cavalry officers and their wives, all of whom had mutual interests, like 11th Hussar Jim Lisley and his wife Dawn, 16th Lancer Geoffrey Brooke, brother-in-law and for many years assistant trainer to Atty Persse, and his sweet wife Betty.

Brownie recalls, 'I was the only one with a small baby. We had no electric light or lamps so I had to wash every nappy by hand. Sarah was six weeks old when we moved up to Brignall Grange about three and a half miles from the town. We had ponies, traps, greyhounds, a dalmatian, horses – it was a lovely place.'

Neville says, 'We had a bit of hunting with the harriers there. There was a wonderful old lady called Mrs Field of Lartington Hall. She never jumped anything. She would get off her horse (she rode side-saddle), hand it over to Jim, who would jump the fence for her while she clambered over. Then he had to heave her up on the other side. She rode a horse with a dipped back, a pure black which looked just like a hearse horse. In fact she called it the Hearse Horse.'

Brownie says, 'She was a good old girl. She came here once in a Rolls-Royce and it ran away down the hill. When you went to her house, you couldn't sit on a chair for Pekineses!'

Early in 1945 Victor and Bunny McCalmont came to join Neville and Brownie. Victor, who belongs to one of the most prominent families in bloodstock breeding and racing during the last century, had served throughout the war with the Royals (Royal Dragoons) and had returned to Barnard Castle before going back to rejoin his regiment in Germany, where he was responsible for running Hanover racecourse.

His son Harry, who runs the Ballylinch Stud, is named after Colonel Harry McCalmont, who was born in 1861 and was a subaltern of sporting tastes serving in the Royal Warwickshire Regiment when, apparently to his surprise, he inherited an immense fortune from a great-uncle. He forthwith transferred to the Scots Guards and decided to indulge his enthusiasm for racing, wisely placing his interests in the experienced hands of Captain Machell.

The best horse that Colonel Harry McCalmont owned was Isinglass, the Triple Crown winner of 1893, who was only once beaten during the four seasons he was in training and, in the latter half of the nineteenth century, won £57,455 in stakes, a total that remained a record until surpassed by Tulyar's earnings in 1952. In the recently built Newmarket luxury housing estate there are McCalmont Way and Isinglass Close.

Harry McCalmont served in the South African War, became Tory MP for Newmarket and died suddenly in 1902. The bulk of his fortune was left to Dermot McCalmont when he was only six years old. After leaving Eton Dermot joined the 7th Hussars and in 1911 won the Grand Military Gold Cup on his own horse Vinegar Hill. The following year his cousin Atty Persse allowed him to buy at cost price a large grey yearling colt by Roi Herode which he had bought for 1300 guineas at the Doncaster Sales – a generous act which Atty always regretted. So Dermot became the owner of that remarkable animal The Tetrarch, probably the fastest horse ever seen on an English racecourse. Unbeaten at two, The Tetrarch developed leg trouble and never raced again. Alistair Fraser, one of the finest vets of the century, has always said, 'The nearer you get to perfection, the more likely something is to go.' This applies to blood vessels and legs particularly. The Tetrarch, as far as anyone can judge, was nearer to perfection than any racehorse ever known.

Dermot McCalmont, Major McCalmont as he was to be known on the Turf, owned two winners of the 2000 Guineas in The Tetrarch's son Tetratema, another grey who, like The Tetrarch, became Champion Sire, and Tetratema's son Mr Jinks, also grey, at that time an unusual colour, who was a stud failure. These great horses are buried on the McCalmonts' glorious estate at Mount Juliet, County Kilkenny. Dermot McCalmont achieved many successes both in Ireland, where his horses were trained by Robert Fetherstonhaugh and later by 'Brud' Fetherstonhaugh, and in England, where, after Atty Persse's retirement in 1953, his horses were trained at Newmarket by Atty's brother-in-law Geoffrey Brooke. A generous and hospitable man, Dermot McCalmont was dedicated to foxhunting and was Master of two packs. For many years he was Master of the Kilkenny and he continued hunting until the year before he died.

Today his eldest son, Major Victor McCalmont, who served with the Royal Dragoons until 1947, has ensured that the famous colours of light blue and scarlet quarter with a white cap have been honoured on the Turf as much as ever. In Kilkenny, where there were at one time a hundred employees on the estate, Victor has proved himself as good and popular a landlord as his father and, as a long-time Steward and Senior Steward of the Turf Club, he has served Irish racing so well that it owes an immense debt to this sporting, conscientious administrator. Under Victor and his attractive wife Bunny, daughter of a Master of Foxhounds and a superb horsewoman, Mount Juliet has remained an oasis in the desert of today's world, a wonderful reminder of times that are gone: pre-war valeting for all guests; breakfast in bed for the women, while the men come down to join Victor, who likes to catch a salmon, on the terrace before fishing. Sadly the salmon are now severely poached at the mouth of the Nore, the foxes are trapped and, as I write, Mount Juliet itself is up for sale.

All this was forty years in the future when, with the war

drawing to its close, Victor married Bunny and came to live with the Crumps in their little cottage while Victor, too, instructed at Barnard Castle. Now, as the Allied armies swept through Belgium and Holland, and into Germany, British racing began to wake up from its sleep.

As soon as war had been declared in September 1939, sports gatherings were prohibited and racing did not resume until the October at Newmarket. For the rest of the season there were also fixtures at Newbury, Thirsk, Stockton and Manchester. Several courses were used for racing in 1940 until, on 19 June, the Jockey Club announced that, after consultation with the government, all racing was suspended until further notice. A fixture list was resumed on 14 September, but the number of horses in training and at stud were drastically reduced. Racing continued throughout the remainder of the war, although in 1942 the number of courses was restricted. A regional system was introduced, whereby racing at Newmarket, with the exception of the substitute classic races and a few other important events, was confined to horses trained there. The Salisbury and Windsor meetings were only for horses trained south of the Trent (Newmarket excluded), and Pontefract and Stockton were used for those trained in the North. Events for two-year-olds dominated the programmes and stayers races were sporadic.

The Second World War affected breeding too, even more adversely than the first, and it was responsible for many changes in stud management. Breeders were urged to reduce their establishments so that pasture could be converted into arable land. When paddocks were ploughed up on the orders of the Ministry of Agriculture, the necessary crowding together of mares and foals greatly increased the risk of infestation by redworm. Breeders had only native stock to consider when normally they would be buying in from abroad. Negotiations took place between the Jockey Club and government departments and what amounted to a gentleman's agreement was effected. Breeders reduced their studs to a minimum and the government arranged a system of rationing – admittedly inadequate, but the best that could be devised. Scales of food rationing were laid down for all types of stock (e.g. broodmares, foals, stallions) at various periods of their stud life. Horses in training were similarly rationed, the management and organization of the system being virtually controlled by Weatherby's offices. The Duke of Norfolk, at that time joint Parliamentary Secretary with Mr Tom Williams (who later became Minister of Agriculture under a Socialist government) and the Minister himself, Robert Hudson, cooperated with Lord Rosebery, who, acting in an official capacity, was an invaluable adviser and ally.

The reduction process was effected largely by culling the older and unprofitable mares and, as a result of this, the whole of the thoroughbred population temporarily diminished. By 1942 the foal population had fallen to 2282 (in 1939 3675 foals had been born).

Noel Murless, who had spent the first half of the war farming at Middleham, told me that he watched a revolution in farming take place on practically every stud farm in the country. Even the smallest breeders were compelled by their local War Agricultural Committee to plough up a proportion of their grasslands, reducing to a minimum the average necessary for maintaining their stock. In the early stages of the war many injustices occurred due to the inability of the committee executives to understand the needs of breeders. In some instances owners were told that they only needed pasture for their stallions, regardless of the fact that in the covering season each breeder had to provide accommodation for around forty mares and their foals. Matters, however, were gradually smoothed out and breeders made the best of what many of them regarded as a bad job.

From the middle of 1942 until the autumn of 1944 there was no jump racing at all. Help was needed to convince austere war-time officialdom that racing and the thoroughbred are essential parts of Britain's heritage. King George VI provided much of that help by leasing top-class yearlings from the National Stud and racing them in the royal colours. By great good fortune among those yearlings in the autumn of 1940 were Big Game and Sun Chariot. Inspired by the

King's example, racing began to make a slow but steady comeback.

National Hunt racing was a very different matter. When the national war effort was intensified grasslands were ploughed up to produce food and every patch of ground, including railway embankments, had to be made productive. The slogan was 'Dig for Victory'. It made good sense, but horses could not be kept without grass. In the rural counties farmers had to dispose of old horses, young horses, broodmares, although somehow they contrived to keep a few favourites. A source which had supplied steeplechasing for more than a hundred years was virtually closed and by 1943 a thoroughbred of this type was a liability, so demanding was it of time and grass. Many good horses were lost in the war years. Those who had been seven years old in 1939, on the edge of their prime and promising great things, were becoming old and stiff and beyond recovery by 1945. The big names of 1939 were already dead or pensioned off.

Good jockeys were lost also. Some, including Frank Furlong, who had won the Grand National on Reynoldstown, were killed on active service. Others lost vital years in the sands of the Middle East and the jungles and prison camps of the Far East. Arthur Thompson, who is to play a big part in this story, was one who had been a prisoner-of-war. By the time the war was over the champions of 1939 were almost forgotten, while those who had been schoolboys were knocking for places in the limelight. The working life of a jump jockey is inevitably much shorter than that of his counterpart on the flat.

When the war in Europe ended racecourses began to open again. Bloodstock sales began to do a good business once more. Those who had been abroad during the six years of the war and who had yearned for British racing came home expecting to find it as they had left it. But there had been a great many changes. There was, for instance, no racing at Ascot until January 1944, vulnerable as it was to bombing action so near to London. Ascot would never really be the same again. Although few realized it, the holocaust had completely altered the social structure of the country. For a while there was sufficient money about to foster the belief that all was just as it had been before, but it was an illusion.

Throughout, although so many of her sons fought in the British Army, Ireland remained obstinately neutral. This was the situation into which one of the greatest steeplechasers of all time had been thrown. Marooned on their tiny island by the war, a whole generation of fine Irish steeplechasers, normally exported to race all over Europe, instead ran furiously against each other for chicken-feed stakes. It is necessary to know this in order to appreciate why Arkle had to win two Cheltenham Gold Cups before Tom Dreaper conceded that 'he might be the Prince's equal'.

The Prince was Prince Regent, who, born in 1935, had been bought as a yearling at Goff's sales by Harry Bonner on behalf of Mr J. V. Rank. At the time the stock of My Prince were carrying all before them. My Prince was leading sire for the third time and his sons had won two Cheltenham Gold Cups and three Grand Nationals in eight years. Two of the Nationals had been won by Reynoldstown, whom Mr Rank could have bought as a young horse but did not on account of his black colour. 'Isn't that the colour of the funeral horses?' say the Irish.

Prince Regent may have been one of the greatest steeple-chasers of all time, but he carried a jinx. He was sent to Bobby Power to be broken, and when the young vet was killed, changing a tyre on the road to the Dublin Horse Show, he was transferred along with several of Mr Rank's other youngsters to Mr Tom Dreaper, then a substantial farmer with a few horses. His education completed, The Prince was sent to England to Gwyn Evans, who controlled the National Hunt side of the Druids' Lodge establishment. Not long afterwards Evans too was killed in a motor accident and Prince Regent sailed back across the Irish Sea to the land of his birth. He returned to Tom Dreaper's Kilsallaghan Farm where he remained until the final two seasons of his great career.

Between 1941 and 1945 he won twelve races in Ireland. These included the 1942 Irish Grand National, in which he carried 12 st 7 lb. He became a legend in his own country, and

65

when he made his first eagerly awaited visit to England he was surrounded by admirers. Nor were his public disappointed in his first major test. He won the 1946 Cheltenham Gold Cup by five lengths. Press and public were eulogistic but Timmy Hyde's post mortem was not. That fine jockey said, 'It took me a moment or two to beat that fellow today, Tom.' Those quiet words meant that trainer and jockey, in the moment of triumph, acknowledged the fact that peace had come too late. The brilliance had gone and Prince Regent, now eleven, was too old to stamp his glory on the English Turf.

Nevertheless, as the crowd flocked back to Aintree in 1946 for the first Grand National since the war, Timmy Hyde, like a champion boxer, would not hear of defeat. Timmy, who had come from the show ring to win on Workman, informed the world that Prince Regent was the greatest horse and would surely be capable of giving 25 lb to Lovely Cottage and of carrying 12 st 5 lb round the 4½ miles of Liverpool.

Lovely Cottage, two years younger than the Prince, was a bay gelding, bred in County Cork, the son of a top-class point-to-point mare. He had made his early appearances in hunter company and during 1943–44 won three chases, including the prestigious Conyngham Cup. In December 1945 he was advertised for sale at £2000 plus £1000 'when he wins a Grand National'. In those days this was a great deal of money, and Lovely Cottage, a most resolute stayer who won the race on merit, has suffered in that the great grief felt by the racing world over the defeat of the gallant Prince Regent has overshadowed his achievement. That advertised price, which was actually paid for him, was a clear indication of his merit. John Morant, who bought him, accepted the contingency and sent the eight-year-old to Tommy Rayson near Winchester, was fully justified.

How good Prince Regent was may be judged from the fact that although he had clearly gone, he almost pulled it off. Throughout the first circuit he promised to justify all hopes and Irish boasts, lying handy to Limestone Edward and dominating the rest in a fashion reminiscent of mighty Troytown. The packed stands, returning to Liverpool after all those dreary blacked-out years, cheered him over the water, then cheered again as he took over from Limestone Edward.

But by now the course was littered with fallen horses. Running loose, they were cantering, lolloping around, seeking ways out. They ran beside Prince Regent, nagging him, checking him, crossing him. Hyde had to shake them off. He rode what amounted to a series of finishes, yet still Prince Regent was in front. He reached the last fence to the old cry, 'He's only got to stand up to win.' He stood up all right, but still he did not win. His ears were flopping, his nostrils flying, tattered banners. His head went down in weariness, and although he went on giving, dredging up the dregs in the fashion of a great horse who will not consider defeat, he could not hold off Lovely Cottage. Thirty-three-year-old Captain Bobby Petre, until recently with the Scots Guards, rode Lovely Cottage as well as any professional. He was the last amateur to ride the winner for nineteen years. The packed stands could not believe what they saw. Dismay and affection mingled as they watched the beaten favourite, calling him home with an admiring roar which made it seem like victory. They were scarcely aware that Jack Finlay had stolen second place from their wonderful hero. Lovely Cottage won by four lengths from Jack Finlay, with Prince Regent an exhausted third. Only three others got round.

This was the atmosphere in which Neville achieved his life's ambition which had been thwarted all those years and started training again. Bunny McCalmont says 'Neville kept a few horses in stables and barns round Barnard Castle. We had such a lot of fun. We would go hunting, with Victor riding an old horse called Chinese Order, Neville on Old Pal and I would ride Blueit, a young horse whom Victor had brought over. It was rather frightening because he was, at that time, an entire colt and suddenly he would kneel down, biting the ground, and throw lumps of turf over his shoulder!'

Neville was already beginning to show his brilliance as a trainer. In the Stand Novices Hurdle (worth £100) on 9 November at Catterick Bridge, Blueit, ridden by Peter Wall, a young man who had been with the Crumps at Upavon, started at 8-1 and duly won his first race over hurdles as a four-year-old by two lengths in the McCalmont colours. 'Major Victor McCalmont, trained N. Crump.' Those words meant so much.

'In fact, I won sixteen races on the flat,' Neville recalls, 'and I had to make up my mind which to do because Brownie said I would wear myself out doing both. So I decided to concentrate on the jumpers. Pity in a way – if I had chosen the flat I might have had a few pennies now.'

Neville and Brownie were looking to the future. They had fallen in love with the North Riding of Yorkshire, its moors and its wonderful, generous people. Twenty miles south of Barnard Castle, across the moors and the other side of Wensleydale, lay the old training centres of Richmond and Middleham. There the Crumps knew that they wanted to settle.

Middleham has a fine tradition of training racehorses. The monks of Jervaulx Abbey probably started the horsebreeding and training that made Middleham a racing centre before Newmarket. The former capital of Wensleydale is only a pretty village now, and the castle that led to its settlement is a ruin in the care of the Ministry of Public Buildings and Works, but in the thirteenth century it was the Windsor of the North. In 1471 it was acquired by Richard III, whose son was born there, and to this day the society which seeks to establish his innocence of the murder of the princes in the Tower still meets in Middleham.

It is just over a hundred years since Dobson Peacock started training at Manor House, Middleham, under the ruined castle walls. Built of old grey stone, like the castle, and backing onto moorland, the stableyard at Middleham's lovely Manor House is unlike any other racing establishment in the world.

In 1869, only a few years before the arrival of Dobson Peacock at Manor House, Pretender walked all the way from here to Epsom to win the Derby for Yorkshire. Tom Dawson's great colt is said to have taken nearly three months to do the journey, but he triumphed. He was the last horse to win the Derby for the North until, as seems only right and proper, a Peacock-trained horse won eighty years later.

One of Dobson's favourite sayings was 'Put your faith in

Yorkshire horses, cricketers, puddings and beef!' He was born on 29 February 1856, nearby at Harmby. The Peacocks had always been substantial yeoman farmers and Dobson's father, Thomas Peacock, bred good horses on that wonderful Yorkshire land, to hunt and show successfully round all the local shows in God's own country. As a young man, Dobson rode a good deal both on the flat and over hurdles in the days when there were many more races for amateurs and when hunters' flat races were popular. He rode out a lot for Harry Hall, who was then training at Spigot Lodge, and he also rode the famous John Osborne's own horse Charlie Boy in a steeplechase at Catterick Bridge in 1877 when, as Dobson remembered, the jockeys had to change in a tent.

John Osborne, a member of a Suffolk family who migrated to Yorkshire, had his first ride in 1846 and his last in 1892. Completely incorruptible, he was for years the idol of Yorkshire. He rode in thirty-eight consecutive Derbys, and in 1869 won the Derby and the 2000 Guineas on Pretender. He rode very short for those days and, because of his style, was known as 'the Old Pusher'. When taxed about the shortness of his leathers he once said, 'It's as much as I can do to ride in the old English style, although I always rode much shorter than Archer, Fordham and other jockeys of my time. But then I had shorter legs, apart from believing in the forward seat, though not to the extreme it has now got.'

John Osborne was a great churchman and for years acted as church warden or sidesman at the little church at Coverham near his Middleham home. When well over eighty his family insisted upon him riding a pony rather than a thoroughbred horse on the moor to superintend the work of the few horses he still had under his charge. He was most indignant but eventually gave way. As late as 1913, however, he rode The Guller the full length of the Chester Cup course on the day before the horse won the big race, and he also gave Mynora her final pipe-opener before she won the 1912 Northumberland Plate.

A virtual tee-totaller and non-smoker, who never swore and was described by a contemporary as 'one of the most honourable and purest-minded men it's ever been my good fortune to meet', Osborne had a great influence on all who knew him and in particular on his special friend, Dobson Peacock.

Dobson Peacock started to train in the early 1880s, but went on riding in public, as an amateur, until 1895, his last mount being Grasp, on which he won the Club Plate at Manchester. At the time that Dobson, a member of a highly respected Yorkshire farming family, started training, trainers were, for the most part, regarded as little better than grooms. Those upper-class sportsmen, the Honourable George Lambton and Atty Persse, deserve the credit for finally breaking the mould, but in his lifetime Old Dob, as he came to be known, by his example did a tremendous amount towards raising the standard of the training profession.

In the years after the First World War there were an increasing number of horses and winners coming from Manor House Stables. The best of his earliest horses was Golden Drop, and possibly the most outstanding horse he trained was Denbigh. Naturally, it was Dobson's greatest ambition to train a Derby and St Leger winner, but the classics eluded him. Something always happened to the animals he thought had rather more than an outsider's chance at Epsom.

In 1932 he achieved the other major ambition of his life by training 100 winners in a season. At that time he had in his yard a good sprinter called Heronslea, who won at Ascot and was twice successful in the Ayr Gold Cup. On a Friday in November 1932 at Manchester's Castle Irwell track Old Dob needed only one more winner when racing started that afternoon to complete his century. He was narrowly beaten in the opening seller, and his next three runners finished down the course. Finally his hundredth winner came when Joe Taylor romped home on Heronslea and the Manchester crowd, going wild with excitement, mobbed the seventy-six-year-old gentleman as though he had won the Derby. His grandson Dick showed me a silver salver bearing the legend: 'Presented to Dobson Peacock in commemoration of his having trained one hundred winners in 1932.' The names of the owners who made the gift include Faversham Ellesmere, Hartington, Hanmer,

Kincald Lennox, Hamilton of Dalziel and Cunningham Jardine.

Although Dobson continued to take an interest in his string and to go up on the moor in his car right to the end of his life, his son Matthew (Matt) virtually took over as trainer for a couple of years before his father's death in 1935.

He took over the training licence when his father died and continued the high tradition of Manor House Stables, accepting, as his father had done, new owners with care and discrimination. I remember him as a famous and much loved Yorkshireman, a very shrewd judge of character who hated humbug and dishonesty. Essentially forthright with no nonsense about him, Matt was a true professional of the highest calibre. He really knew his job. One day at Edinburgh, when I was a schoolboy, he marked my card for me, giving me four horses which he said would win. These were not just tips. He told me, 'They will win' – and they did.

During the First World War Matt served in the Yorkshire Hussars and became the regiment's farrier major. In those days the farrier major was on a par with the regimental sergeant major. If the latter looked after the men, then the farrier major was responsible for the 600 horses in the regiment. He was more than just the vet's right-hand man. In many respects he was the vet.

Like his father, who won no fewer than six Northumberland Plates, Matt was always to be feared in the big northern races and, indeed, when he made the journey to the south-country meetings. It was then, after an Ascot or Newmarket meeting, that Matt would produce his famous farewell – 'Goodbye. Now I'm off back to England!' In four seasons between 1936 and 1939 he had a larger number of winners than any other trainer, although he never headed the list based on aggregate stakes won.

During the Second World War, when Matt commanded the Home Guard at Middleham, racing was restricted to Stockton and Pontefract. So Matt branched out. His son Dick said, 'My father had a fair amount of success in Ireland just before the war, winning the Irish Oaks and Leger, in addition to big races like the Cambridgeshire and the National Produce Stakes. Owenstown won the Ulster Derby and later the Ebor. I think my father regarded Merry Matthew as one of the best horses he trained and he was sorry that the horse was not entered in the Derby of his year.' Merry Matthew, who won the Chester Vase, was by Truculent out of Bonny Brighteyes.

Great trainer that he was, Matt never gambled, and to understand the effects which the devastating year of 1945 had upon him it is necessary to understand the man. When he died in 1951 *The Times* obituary read:

> It is as though a great tree has fallen and the landscapes of race meetings will never again be quite the same. The knowledge that his rugged figure, crowned by his well-known, well-worn Homburg hat, which assumed a shape entirely its own, pulled sharply down over his keen kindly eyes and bold features will never again be seen, nor the voice be heard giving final instructions (in the unmistakable Yorkshire tongue) to a jockey, or telling an owner the blunt truth about his horse, or an owner's wife not to bet too high – these sad facts are hard to realize. He has left his lovely Wensleydale where he will be remembered with faithful affection as a master and a friend whose high standards of efficiency were matched by his generosity and kindness which found expression in a lifetime of kind acts. He could stand no humbug or dishonesty in any form. Downright in speech, courageous in action, he meant what he said, and he said what he meant in no uncertain terms. His shrewd, keen sense of humour made his company a delight and beneath his bluff, forthright manner his great heart could be touched by real compassion.

Such was the character of the man at the heart of one of the great Turf dramas of the century, which began when Lord Glanely was killed in an air raid in 1942. A Cardiff shipowner, he was a vigorous, forceful personality and was raised to the peerage in 1918. After the First World War he became an owner and breeder on a very lavish scale and spent quite a fortune on bloodstock. On the racecourse he was irreverently but affectionately known as 'Guts and Gaiters'. He won the 1919 Derby with Grand Parade. Other notable winners were Rose of England (Oaks), Colombo (2000 Guineas), Singapore

(St Leger), Chumleigh (St Leger) and Dancing Time (1000 Guineas).

On his death, Lord Glanely's bloodstock was offered for sale and Matt Peacock bought the mare Rosy Legend in foal to Nearco for Sir Eric Ohlson, a shipping magnate from Hull. A daughter of Dark Legend, Rosy Legend had been foaled in France in 1931. The mare went back to the farm Ohlson had bought near Middleham and in due course produced a lovely dark bay colt. Matt Peacock, who, like his father, had always been a successful breeder in his own right and supervised Ohlson's stud farm, raised the foal and took him into training as a yearling.

Named Dante, he became the outstanding two-year-old of 1944, winning the Coventry and Middle Park and finishing up as a warm favourite for the classics of 1945. A beautiful, commanding horse of supreme quality, he wintered really well and by the spring of 1945 was a truly magnificent example of the thoroughbred. It looked more and more certain that Matt would achieve the distinction of winning the first Derby gained by a Yorkshire stable since Pretender won in 1869. But the occasional slight clouding in one of the colt's eyes gave the trainer cause for concern.

Today, thanks to antibiotics, periodic ophthalmia, or moon blindness as it is called, is much rarer than it was in the forties. This disease causes inflammation of the tissues inside the eyeball and this is usually the only sign that the horse is infected with the bacteria leptospirosis. The first indication of ophthalmia is when one eye closes up and a few tears flow onto the face. This resembles any slight damage to the eye, but with periodic ophthalmia inspection with an ophthalmoscope shows that the fluid in the front of the eye is cloudy, so that the lens and the back of the eye cannot be seen. The other eye may be affected to some degree or not at all.

The inflammation subsides within a week or ten days, though the ophthalmoscope may show that the cells which cause the clouding in front of the lens have settled as a white deposit low down in the eye, and the pupil may be a little misshapen. The upper eyelid, instead of forming a smooth

73

curve, develops a central peak, giving the eye a slightly triangular appearance. But the disease is likely to recur after an interval of a few weeks, although not as regularly as the stable name of moon blindness might imply. The attacks may recur again and again, each one leaving the eye in a worse state. The eyeball sinks a little, the lens becomes cloudy, the pupil deformed and the cornea opaque, rendering the eye quite useless. Both eyes are usually affected by these later attacks and the horse eventually becomes blind. This is what happened to the Derby favourite throughout 1945.

Billy Nevett, the Manor House jockey, rode Dante in all his races. In the 2000 Guineas the colt looked certain to win until he threw up his head. He was beaten by a neck by Court Martial. It was said at the time that a bit of mud had flown up and hit him in the eye. Dick Peacock said bluntly, 'It didn't. He was blind.'

Nevett had won the Derby in 1941 and 1944 on Owen Tudor and Ocean Swell. In 1945 the classic was still run at Newmarket. Dante, back to his best, won comfortably by two lengths from Midas, with Court Martial a head away third. When a friend congratulated Matt on the triumph, his only comment was, 'Aye, he goes a bit.'

Some measure of the effect of Dante's victory in Yorkshire can be gauged by the unveiling of a plaque on a railway horsebox sponsored by the London North Eastern Railway, which read: 'Dante, Sir Eric Ohlson's colt, trained by Matthew J. Peacock, travelled in this box from Middleham to Newmarket and back to win the Derby, 1945.' But this happy day started the unhappiest period in Matthew Peacock's life – a period which was to contribute to his death six years later.

After winning the 1945 Derby Dante became hot favourite for the St Leger. It was reported that over £1 million worth of bets had been placed on the Yorkshire-trained colt, but, unbeknown to press and public, the moon blindness that had plagued him throughout his three-year-old career was gradually getting worse.

Dick Peacock, looking back, said: 'He was a really high-class horse, a brilliant colt who would definitely have won the

Leger. They worked him up on High Moor and he got two miles well. It was an extraordinary thing for a horse of such brilliant speed to get that distance.' Perhaps Dante was the nearest approach to his sire Nearco, who, in the opinion of Etienne Pollet, was the greatest horse that he had ever seen.

As the blindness intensified Matt Peacock, who had achieved quite a feat of training by keeping his horse sound enough to win the Derby, realized that there was no question of him running in the St Leger. Never a gambler and always the most honest member of his profession, Matt's reaction was to tell the public as soon as he had decided that the horse could not, under any circumstances, run at Doncaster. Dick said, 'He wanted to tell the papers that Dante would not run in the Leger because he knew that the horse's sight was getting worse.' Unfortunately there were pressures on Matt that forced him to delay his announcement.

The rumours about the favourite began to spread. There was no mention of the blindness but he was said to be suffering from muscular trouble after a gallop at the beginning of August. Crowds of punters and reporters filled the Black Swan at Leyburn trying to get news of the horse, going out in the early morning to watch for Dante at work. They seldom saw the colt, who had been backed with thousands of pounds ante-post, both before and after the Derby. He was in his box behind the Manor House and was blind.

Dick Peacock's widow, Lenny, says, 'It was so embarrassing that it nearly killed Dick's father. With the telephone calls and the press always on the doorstep, he couldn't sleep at night. He had been put in a desperately invidious position. He, a man who never gambled and who had told the truth all his life, was being made to look like a gambler and a liar. When people telephoned him, he didn't know what to do; he didn't want to lie but he was not allowed to tell the truth.'

Dante was eventually scratched from the St Leger on the evening of 24 August. And, as though the sickness and blindness of his beloved Derby-winning colt were not enough, all the badgering and hypocrisy were so completely alien to Matt that they nearly broke the old man's heart.

Two years earlier Dante had failed to fetch his reserve at the yearling sales. Now his full brother came up at those same sales and Matt Peacock had 27,000 guineas to spend on him for a brewer called John Hamer. But after a notorious battle between the Maharajah of Baroda and Charles Tremayne, a very popular owner and sportsman, the colt was knocked down to Baroda for 28,000 guineas, a record which was to stand for many years. Trained by Sam Armstrong and named Sayajirao, he became a very good horse and, ironically, went on to win the St Leger.

It is now said that Dante, who was undefeated in his six two-year-old starts, showed his eye affliction for the first time just a few days before the 2000 Guineas and it is thought by some that he might have become accustomed to the weakness in his eye by the time he won the Derby. After leaving Middleham he never ran again, and was retired to stud where he soon became totally blind.

As a sire he was a qualified success. He got a fair number of winners but a good many of his off-spring were distinctly temperamental. The best horse he sired was Darius, winner of the 2000 Guineas and the Eclipse Stakes. Dante himself died in 1956.

On Matt Peacock's death in 1951, Dick took over at Manor House. In 1953 he married Lenny Quinlan, who is from an old Irish racing family and whose sister is married to Peter Nelson. Between them for more than thirty years they carried on the tradition of the Peacocks of Middleham with proud success, both on the racecourse and on the stud which forms part of the 500 acres that Dick farmed as his grandfather and father had done. When Dick died recently, mourners from far and wide waited in the fourteenth-century church of Sts Mary and Alkelda, while the hearse carrying his coffin stood according to tradition for ten minutes outside the Manor House, allowing the villagers to bid their own personal farewells to the last of the Peacocks.

5

From his first little hurdle victory with Blueit at Catterick Bridge on 9 November 1945 Neville never looked back. Success brought more horses and the number of winners increased. First Neville had to overcome one big hurdle himself, the Master of Middleham. 'When I first met old Matt Peacock he said, "I don't like your bloody jumping 'osses". So I said, "Oh, I'm very sorry." His old eyes twinkled and he said, "Behave yourself and you'll be all right."'

There was one more brush with the great man. Neville had to build schooling fences and put up hurdles by the gallops on Low Moor. 'There were no jumps at all. Nothing,' he says. 'Matt said, "I'm not having bloody jumpers 'ere!" But he soon changed his mind and we got on famously together after that.'

Matt even got on well with Neville's father following an initial skirmish. 'They were looking at a horse and Matt said, "Get down and feel his legs." My old man said, "No. I don't want to feel his legs," and blew Matt's head off. But then they both laughed, went off to the pub and had a drink together!'

Brownie remembers the day when Matt Peacock was coming back from Liverpool, driven by Roland Handley, who looked after the old man's car. 'The road was flooded,' she says, 'and suddenly they ran into a flood, and old Roland said, "I think we'll have to turn back, Mr Peacock." "No, go on Roland. I want my tea," said Matt. Then suddenly he shouted "Stop! Stop! It's up to me assholes!" He was actually sitting in the water.

'I remember another lovely story when the old man knew that he wasn't getting as many eggs from his hens as he should. One day he was standing looking out of the window, when he saw a little apprentice boy coming through the hole through which the hens entered the hen house. So he went down and said, "Come here, boy!" The terrified little lad was holding a couple of eggs in his hand and Matt said, "Are you 'ungry, lad?" The little boy said, "Yes, Mr Peacock." So Matt gave him half a crown and told him to go and buy some sandwiches instead of giving him the anticipated beating.'

Neville chuckles. 'There was a wonderful day at Newmarket sales. An old woman said, "Oh, Mr Peacock, I'd love your opinion on this yearling I've just bought." The old man looked at the animal and said, "Hey, ain't the old bugger fat!" That's all he said.'

Peter Wall, who had been with the Crumps at Upavon and had ridden Blueit, had now disappeared from the scene. Jack Bissill rode quite a few for Neville, but then came a transformation when the Crumps were joined by Arthur Thompson, a splendid Irish horseman.

Arthur told me, 'I was born in Carlow but I have spent as much time in England as in Ireland. My father was a watchmaker who knew nothing at all about horses. My mother died when I was about five so I was sent off to an aunt in the country, and I lived with her. She had a son who used to ride in England. He was away when I arrived, but shortly he came back and started working for the Alexanders, a well liked and well known sporting family. He was still with them when he was eighty-one. He was very good to me. He used to buy me breeches and so on. Paddy Claxton was his name, and, it was during the short period when he was working with the Curwens near Gowran in Kilkenny that he got me to serve my time with them. I was about thirteen when I was apprenticed there. It was a tough life. I had very little to eat and I was exceptionally small at that time. People used to say, "You won't have any trouble with your weight." Then, when I was about seventeen, I went from around 7 stone up to 11 stone just like that. I got bigger and bigger. Later on I had a tough time keeping my weight down when I was in England. I hardly ate at all.

'My first ride was a winner, a little mare called Good Thing in a mile and a half contest at Mallow. I weighed 4 stone! For two or three years I was Champion Apprentice in Ireland. I was riding everything – on the flat, over hurdles and fences. I never won anything great on the flat, mostly races worth £21 to the winner!

'It was not until 1936 that I rode in England. When my weight went up there was no point in staying in Ireland because the handicap weights were too light – even the bottom weight of 9 st 7 lb was far too light for me. So I thought I would chance my luck going to England and take it up from there. So I went first to Johnny Harper and rode about sixteen winners for him. I think that in the first year that I was with him he had only ten horses. Then I went to work for Matt Peacock in Middleham for four months. I stayed in the village and moved over to Colonel Wilfred Lyde. He had quite a few horses but they were not exactly great. Now I was really in the jumping scene. I was much too heavy for the flat, 10 stone but not claiming! And, of course, then came the war. Wilfred Lyde had to stop training as he was called up as a soldier. At this time I did not know who Neville Crump was.

'The Army was good to me. My sister died and they let me come home to see her buried. They even let me go to the odd meetings on a Saturday to ride. I joined the Northumberland Fusiliers, a very fine regiment indeed. I had a good time in the Army. I thought, and still do think, that if ever I had a son, that would be the place I would put him. I would make him a soldier in the British Army.

'I went into the Army in March 1940. By August I was on the boat to the Middle East. Of course, when the fighting started in the desert, it was towards the end of December and I was mixed up in it. We landed in Suez and went down to Ismalia. We were there for only a fortnight before we were sent into the desert. At that time we were the only machine gunners in the desert and we were at everyone's beck and call.

'We went right across to Benghazi. There we joined up with the Australian Army. We were getting ready to go on to Tripoli when Rommel and the Germans came on the scene again and there was one hell of a chase back across the desert. The Germans carried on and left us behind. We managed to get hold of an Italian gun truck, loaded it up and started off. At Tobruk the Germans had us completely surrounded – they must have thought we were Italians because we drove straight through their lines! I was in Tobruk right through the siege. Then, when the siege was lifted, we went back to Cairo. My word, what a do there was then! Some of the lads had not drawn any money for a year and a half and the place was in a shambles at night! After a rest we were called back up the desert because there was more trouble. We were captured at Knightsbridge. We ran into a German tank regiment and that was the end. We were taken to Tripoli and put on a boat for Italy. We stayed there for about a week and then they sent us off to a place near Rome and then we were spread among various little prisoner-of-war camps.

'We were very weak. The Italians had not given us anything to eat. Fifteen thousand of us went in and I think 1300 died of malnutrition. There was nothing to eat. We were being looked after by the Italians and we were genuinely starving. They were much worse than the Germans. If any of the lads strayed near the barbed-wire perimeter fence the Italians would walk up behind him and shoot him through the back of the head. My weight went down from 11 stone to 7 stone. You could not escape because you could not walk. In order to stand you had to edge yourself up and down using a wall.

'Then we were taken off to Germany. First, for about three months in Stalag HC and then to a camp near Berlin. This was much better. The Germans gave you a chance to live and to keep yourself clean – there was always water. Here at last we received regular Red Cross parcels containing welcome things like tea. This was great. We would use the tea, dry it out in the sun, put it back in its packet, seal it up and bargain with the guards for bread rolls!'

Arthur was a prisoner for three years. In the spring of 1945 the Germans fled as the Russians advanced and the camp broke up. 'We went down into the local village. The scene that met our eyes was sickening, horrifying. As they advanced, the Russians had destroyed everything. They had laid waste the land and shot every living creature. The roads were littered with dead people, pigs and cattle. Other frightened, bewildered civilians were wandering about aimlessly. With an Australian fellow prisoner we stopped and asked where we could get some rations. They told us where the ration dump was, but warned that it was teaming with Russians. Nevertheless we went down and helped ourselves to a few of the necessities of life. The Russians were getting more than a little rowdy because they'd had too much to drink. My Aussie friend and I decided that we ought to get out of there as quickly as possible and we found a Russian colonel who wanted us to go to Russia!

'That decided us. On no account were we staying. We found some bicycles and pedalled like hell! We pedalled through villages with all the people hanging out of their windows, wondering what was going to happen. Eventually we ran into a French camp, but they too were unfriendly and would not help us to cross the river to the Americans. We had to get out. We managed that all right, but with planes flying overhead all the time we were pretty worried. With the aid of a few buses which were still running, we got down to the river, seized a boat and got across to the American side. The Yanks were friendly and very efficient. They gave us food and soon flew us back. I arrived back in England in June 1945.

'Of course, the war in the Far East was still on, and so, far from being demobilized right away, I had to rejoin the Army and start intensive training again. I ended up in Wales, where I was eventually demobbed.

'As soon as I left the Army I went back to Middleham and started riding a few horses out. By now my weight had gone up to 11 st 7 lb, which shows the trouble I was always to have keeping it down. I had to get down to around the 10-stone mark if I wanted to get plenty of riding. However, I went back to Colonel Wilfred Lyde and worked really hard. Neville Crump was already in Middleham with about half a dozen horses, but I only knew him to say hello.

'Then, on 3 November 1945, I went racing at Wetherby just on spec. It was a full eight-race card and I was sure I would find someone there I knew. There wasn't a single person at that meeting whom I had known before the war. It just shows how the scene had changed. I met a chap called Jack Lynn who used to ride quite a bit at that time and I was standing chatting with him at the door of the dressing room when Clifford Nicholson came up.'

Clifford Nicholson, who died in 1972, was one of the most successful farmers in Lincolnshire and also in Natal. He had served in the Life Guards in the First World War and was a long-standing patron of National Hunt racing. He was a successful breeder, owner and, for a short time, trainer and a founder of the Injured Jockeys' Fund. It was always his ambition to win the Grand National but he never achieved it, although four of his chasers won over fences at Aintree and in 1946 his Limestone Edward finished sixth in the National. In the last fifteen years of his life Mr Nicholson became increasingly keen on flat racing and expanded his Limestone Stud in Lincolnshire and his Tara Stud in County Meath, importing a number of stallions from abroad, primarily from Italy. But at this period, immediately after the Second World War, his interests were still very much with his first love, National Hunt racing. He was regularly in the lists of leading owners (five times between 1948–49 and 1958–59), his best season being 1955–56, when he was second with thirteen races worth £10,069. The best horses that he owned were the Champion Hurdler of 1956, Doorknocker, whom he bred, The Heron, Storm Head, Witty and Billykin, whom he trained himself to win the Stanley Chase at Liverpool in 1947. So it was a wonderful stroke of good fortune when the tall, smiling owner–trainer came up to Arthur outside the Wetherby weighing room.

'His jockey had been hurt and he wanted someone to ride his horses,' says Arthur. 'It was lucky I had brought my breeches and boots with me, just in case! He told me that he had two runners that day and I could ride them both. The first was Group Leader on whom I finished close-up fifth in the Novice Chase and the second was Lavenham in the Three Mile Chase. We started favourite and, taking the lead at the last, ran on to win by five lengths from Jack Finlay, who was to be runner-up to Lovely Cottage in the Grand National four months later.'

Lavenham was subsequently disqualified for carrying the wrong weight but it did not matter. Arthur was back where he belonged, in the winner's enclosure.

6

One of the most famous partnerships in post-war National Hunt history, comparable to that between Ryan Price and Fred Winter, started quietly at Southwell on 12 April 1946.

Southwell is one of the smaller country courses which is essential to the professional element in British racing. A slightly better Midlands equivalent of Sedgefield, a left-handed 1¾-miles triangle with seven fences to a circuit. It is, however, suitable for any kind of horse because the course is easy and the bends are not too sharp. The run-in from the last is 250 yards. Like Sedgefield, it is hell in the rain, and the amenities, although improved in recent years, were not then worthy of the name. It was certainly no place to bring an owner unless you were certain that he would have a winner.

In 1946, and indeed for far too long after the war, the prizemoney at such courses was little short of scandalous. The norm for both chases and hurdle races was a £100 plate, which, after deductions for second and third, finished up as £69 to the winner. As for the jockeys who risked life and limb in all conditions, they received £3 per ride. 'A pound a mile,' as Gerry Wilson would say going out for a 3-mile chase. Looking at the list of jockeys riding at that little Southwell meeting forty years ago I find Tim Molony, the tough, thickset, cheerful Irish star, who was to be Champion Jockey five times and whom his brother jockeys called the 'Rubber Man'. In his entire career this remarkable horseman suffered only one bad fall, when he was forced to retire with a broken thigh at Uttoxeter in 1958. 'I never believed in getting off too soon,' he said. 'I always reckon to ride my horse right into the ground – to the point of no return – before letting myself go. You don't have so far to fall!' Would that many of today's jump jockeys, who seem to take a 'voluntary' or 'dismount prematurely' at the slightest mistake by their horse, possessed the same brand of horsemanship.

Then there was that fine stylist 'Frenchie' Nicholson, later to be known as an outstanding instructor of young jockeys, and, recently demobilized from wartime service with the 'Skins', the Inniskilling Dragoon Guards, both Jack Bissill and Bryan Marshall, another superb horseman and future champion. Arthur says, 'Jack Bissill was riding Neville Crump's few horses at the time. He was supposed to be riding Hill Vixen, a novice chaser who had never run in this country, but he fell and broke his collarbone. So Neville offered me the ride on the mare and I won at 20–1. She was a good horse.'

Even after this success Arthur did not immediately team up with Neville. 'I had been having a lot of falls and my wife Enid, whom I had married in 1937, had to bandage me up every morning,' he says. 'At that time even from schooling I used to be black and blue. I just seemed to keep falling and it went on for ages. Eventually Neville said I could ride his horses for him. As soon as I started for him in the 1946–47 season I knew I was on my way. That season I rode eighteen winners and the score improved every year from then on.'

They were all coming back. Bill Smith, a fine horseman and horsemaster, who now, at the age of fifty-nine, has a nice yard close at hand, was one of Neville's very first lads. 'I was in the Second Battalion of the Green Howards in Calcutta,' he says. 'Before the war I had served my apprenticeship with Harry Peacock at Richmond. When I was demobilized I tried another yard in Middleham but then went to Captain Crump and really enjoyed it. He was a hard man to work for but he was scrupulously fair. He loved his horses. He would always ask me what I thought about the horses and I would tell him. I got on well with him. I'll tell you something, none of these chaps who train today could train like him. They don't have the ability to train in that way. He pays tremendous attention to detail and gets his horses supremely fit steadily and quietly. He never gallops them a lot. Although he may have changed his system a little, we used to go round the roads for two hours. I have seen him take a large string of horses that were just coming ready, each lot round the roads for five to six weeks. Ten to fourteen miles a morning, solid walking and trotting. He never put any strain on the legs. These fellows today either couldn't or wouldn't train horses to put on that sort of condition.'

Every trainer needs at least one good horse who will catch the fancy of the public and of the racing world to establish him. Noel Murless over at Hambleton on the other side of Thirsk was making his name with Closeburn, Oros, Junius and Sejanus. For his exact contemporary Neville Crump the horse that made him came from a strange source.

At the time that Arthur Thompson joined Neville, Sir Hervey Bruce, of the Royal Scots Greys, who was adjutant at Catterick, acquired a point-to-point mare called Sheila's Cottage. Foaled in 1939 and registered in Miss Prior's Half-Bred Stud Book, she was by the great Cottage out of a mare called Sheila II. In those days every jumper or potential jumper was supposed to be by Cottage, just as today they are alleged to be by Deep Run. Hervey, who was later to learn his job with his flat trainer, Sam Armstrong, before taking up the profession himself with considerable success in South Africa, bought the big powerful bay mare for £250. By some accounts she is said to have won a point-to-point, but Arthur Thompson doubts this because she was too much of a handful even for a professional, let alone an amateur, and Hervey was not an outstanding horseman. Neville says, 'Tim Molony came down here one day and rode her out. He told me afterwards, "That's the only horse that has pissed off with me at the trot!"'

Arthur, highly professional and tremendously strong like Tim, says, 'As far as I was concerned, Sheila's Cottage was always an ordeal. Walking up the straight before a race, she would run away with you. She was terrible. She used to put her head so far down that you could not get near it and ended up holding the buckle of the reins. And God, she was vicious! I think that when she was in the Army the soldiers had knocked her about.' It is a fact that certain evil-minded soldiers would deliberately put on an officer's Sam Browne belt and knock a horse about. If this was done often enough the horse would learn to resent officers. It was a cruel ploy, but it worked.

Arthur continues with pride and the sort of affection that one reserves for really naughty children, 'Ah, she was a good mare. Nobody else could ride her. The first time I rode her was at Carlisle in a three-mile novice chase. She broke every fence on the racecourse. She galloped through everything. Even then she finished third. I did not know how I was going to stop with her, so I held the back and the front arch of the saddle. She finished a good third.'

The next time she ran was against more experienced horses in an open 3-mile chase at Haydock on 30 November. Haydock Park, a left-handed oval circuit of 1 mile 5 furlongs, is one of the best courses in the country for flat and for jumping. It is situated within a stone's throw of the M6 motorway and equidistant from Liverpool and Manchester, just off the East Lancs Road. The crowds that attend every meeting are proof of its good racing and its accessibility.

The course is generally flat and the turns are good. It is ideal for any kind of horse, particularly the long-striding, galloping sort like Sheila's Cottage. Moreover, since from the turn into the 4½-furlong straight to the winning post you are always just on the collar, it takes some getting.

Haydock's jumping track is dramatic. In common with many other trainers, I believe that we are playing a confidence trick on horses if we run them at Aintree without running them first at Haydock. The first time that the average racehorse knows what a drop fence means is when he finds himself hurtling over Becher's and looks down to find nothing below him. Haydock remedies this with two nice drop fences in the back stretch. This means that staying races at Haydock are good trials for the Grand National. The course is deservedly popular with owners, trainers, jockeys, horses and stable lads alike.

In those days, even apart from the drops, the fences were big, black and strong and Sheila's Cottage had only had one race under Rules in her life. Arthur says, 'You know what the fences are like at Haydock. I knew she hadn't an awful lot of speed but she could gallop all day. She won in a canter. The ground was heavy and it was a good field. But it was fatal if anything came up beside her and touched her. They would invariably end up on the floor. She was a tank!

'After that day at Carlisle when there were splinters flying all around us, she never hit a fence. She may have fallen by taking a wrong stride but she never hit a fence again.'

A week later Arthur and Sheila's Cottage appeared in the 3-mile Badsworth Chase at Doncaster. The mare ran very well again and, giving 5 lb to the winner, was runner-up to a useful chaser called Russian Lynx.

She went back to Haydock – Neville was making sure that she understood drop fences – on 3 January for the big race of the day, the Gerard Handicap Chase over 3½ miles. She made all the running and won unchallenged by eight lengths.

Here we have a remarkable insight into the genius – and I use the word advisedly – of the trainer, who had only just started again with a few horses but who decided to run a novice in the greatest test of them all, the Grand National. Sheila's Cottage had no more races until 29 March at Aintree.

At the request of Clement Attlee's Government, the race was held on a Saturday. With fifty-seven runners, it was the biggest field since Gregalach had won in 1929. It was the second biggest field in the history of the National. The going was all mud. In the early part of the year, during the terrible winter, Neville had taken the horses to Redcar for more than a month. The sands and his knowledge of how to use them had done Sheila's Cottage a power of good. The icy conditions had only broken a fortnight before the Liverpool meeting. Weeks of snow and frost had been followed by relentless rain. Training schedules had been interrupted and preliminary races had been cancelled. Any fully fit horse must have had a chance. Conditions were right for another fluke result and the Irish horse Caughoo provided it at 100–1.

It must have seemed to Tom Dreaper that handicappers were quite ruthless, but still he brought back Prince Regent with 12 st 7 lb, a hideous weight to carry for 4½ miles in bottomless going over the biggest and toughest fences in the world. Fourteen-year-old Bogskar was trying again. So was fifteen-year-old MacMoffat, the gallant Scottish horse who was runner-up in 1939 and 1940.

From the stands only part of the course could be seen and spectators on the far side, huddled near Becher's and Valentine's, relied on portable radios and Raymond Glendenning to tell them what was happening. Revelry and EP fell at the first, Bullington and Michael's Pearl at the third, where Prince Regent blundered but kept his feet; Timmy Hyde, limpet-like as ever, was still the great horse's pilot. Day Dreams was pulled up as they came to Becher's for the first time. Linthill dropped out. There were many fallers, including Bogskar, MacMoffat, First of the Dandies, Klaxton and Bomber Command. Sheila's Cottage was going really well until, as they jumped the third last fence first time round, the twelfth in the race, she was brought down.

Prince Regent was there with a chance as they negotiated Becher's for the second time, but after that he struggled in the mud. Caughoo, with a weight advantage of 25 lb, went on with another Irish lightweight Lough Conn. Lord Bicester's magnificent jumper Silver Fame, thrown into the handicap with only 10 st 12 lb, which he would never have again, and ridden by the previous winning jockey, Captain Bobby Petre, was in a challenging position three out where he was impeded and brought down by Tulyra. Caughoo jumped the last in front, while rain-drenched spectators tried to identify his colours and to guess his name. Afterwards many were to speculate whether he had gone around twice or had hidden in the mist for one round. 'Didn't he only go round the once?' is the question that will always be asked. The public were still guessing as he ran home twenty lengths ahead of Lough Conn. At the last Prince Regent promised to be third for the second time but Kami, ridden by amateur John Hislop, squeezed the weary favourite out of third place.

Caughoo, only the third 100–1 winner in the history of the race, had won two Ulster Grand Nationals and had never fallen. More important, he had had the luck to be prepared on

Portmarnock sands, far from the snow and mud which had frustrated English trainers.

Arthur Thompson says, 'Sheila's Cottage would undoubtedly have won if I could have stopped with her. A horse ran into her at the third last fence, first time round and knocked me off. She fell over the ditch at the back of the fence, got up and went on.' Riderless, she jumped every fence and passed the winning post in front.

Three weeks later Neville decided to run the mare again, this time in the Scottish Grand National at Bogside, a race which he was to make his own. Arthur says, 'I was right there at the third last and, although it was a top-class field in that three mile seven furlong race, Sheila's Cottage was obviously going to win but the fence was down a little hill. The mare was going too fast and I was driving her too hard. As she landed she lost her footing and fell.' But that was not the end of her. Only Sheila's Cottage could do what she did then. She galloped into the sea, swam across the inlet, and it was not until midnight that Neville retrieved her from the police station. She arrived back at the stables at one o'clock in the morning, scratched and battered, with bits of skin hanging off her.

Neville describes that extraordinary season. 'I had only half a dozen horses in the yard. Things did not start too well and that first winter was hell – snow everywhere and we had no idea what we were doing. We had taken the horses up to Redcar and galloped them too much – and we drank too much! We made a right mess of the whole thing!

'Sheila's Cottage was an absolute swine, a real old brute. She would bite and kick anybody, but we soon found out that she knew what she was about on the racecourse. Sir Hervey Bruce was so delighted with her performances that early next season we set out for Cheltenham and the four-mile Stayers Handicap on 30 December. Hervey, who gambled a bit, asked if I thought she would win at Cheltenham. I said, "No, I don't think so. She will be placed." Sadly Hervey did not take me at my word. She finished third after starting 4–1 favourite and my owner came up to me afterwards saying, "Christ, I've done my dough – I'll have to sell the horse."'

Neville had a buyer waiting. Old John Procter had asked him to find a horse for the National. Brownie says, 'Procter owned three trawlers, a pub in Lincolnshire, had a leg in an iron and drank brandy!'

Arthur says, 'We had gone from Cheltenham to Manchester where we were staying at the Midland. The telephone rang and it was Hervey Bruce saying that he had to sell the mare. He wanted £3500 for her. Neville telephoned Procter, who said he would buy the mare for that price if she won the next day. She did not win, but he bought her just the same.'

Neville continues, 'It was very sad for Hervey to lose the horse, but John Procter paid him for her and the first time out in his colours she ran third at Haydock. She then finished fifth in the Great Yorkshire Chase at Doncaster in February where the track was too fast for her. The next stop was Aintree and the Grand National on 20 March – a day that was to change my life.

'Sheila's Cottage started at 50–1 in a field of forty-three and that seemed a fair reflection of her chance at the time, although I had never doubted her ability to stay the four and a half mile course. Nor had I any doubt about the ability of my jockey Arthur Thompson. He knew his way round Aintree backwards. He always went round the inside and liked to be up there from the start – he was the ideal man for the job.

'My new owner was, shall we say, a bit different. Before the National he was full of brandy and shaking like a leaf. There's a large drain at the end where you walk into Liverpool and there, as I arrived at about midday, was Procter, sitting on his shooting stick being sick into the drain. Fulke Walwyn came up to me and said, "A nice new owner you've got!"

'A few nights earlier, when John Procter was in his pub, the Lord Nelson at Brig, all the locals wanted to have a bet on Sheila's Cottage. They asked him, "Go on, John, put this money on your horse for us." He said, "No, I'll stand your bet."'

Almost every Grand National has its bad-luck stories. The Queen Mother, Peter Cazalet and Dick Francis were to suffer one eight years on and Neville himself thirteen years later.

Now the bad-luck stories belonged to Eddie Reavey, rider of Zahia, and to Lord Mildmay, probably the most popular man on the Turf at the time. Anthony Mildmay had inherited the title Lord Mildmay of Flete and, after war service with the Welsh Guards and the Guards Armoured Division, had come back to England determined to establish a string of useful steeplechasers. His partner was Peter Cazalet. Their stables were at Fairlawne, the beautiful Cazalet home in Kent. This was the team which, with Edward Paget and Harry Whiteman, had been at Russley Park before the war. Now, their shared ambition was to win the Grand National with Mildmay riding.

Tall and frail-looking, with a pale, sensitive face and sad eyes, Anthony Mildmay was by no means a natural athlete or even a natural horseman. Yet by determination and physical discipline he made himself a thoroughly proficient amateur rider, able to compete on level terms with the leading professionals of his age, while his courage, example, courtesy and the sheer magnetism of his personality made him one of the best-loved figures in the history of steeplechasing. When he died in May 1950, seemingly inexplicably, people far beyond his immediate circle felt bereaved. Their emotion was best caught by *The Times*, which called him 'the last of the Corinthians' and wrote: 'There never was a harder rider, a better loser or a more popular winner, and though he always valued the race more than the victory and the victory more than the prize, he would perhaps not have disdained the reward which he has won which is a kind of immortality among the English.'

He rode his first winner in 1933 on Good Shot. In 1936 his father bought Davy Jones to ride in the National. The horse was tubed and was thought moreover to have distinct limitations on his stamina, but he was a safe jumper, likely to give an amateur a good ride. The pair started at 100–1 and, with nothing to lose, set out to make the running. As we have seen earlier, they were still in the lead approaching the second last but, as they landed, the brand new reins parted at the buckle. With his steering gone, Davy Jones ran out at the last, leaving Fulke Walwyn to win at his leisure. Anthony Mildmay had deliberately not tied a knot in his reins because, he said, 'Davy had such a tremendously long neck and I needed the full extent of rein for those drop fences.'

After serving in the war in the Welsh Guards, Anthony Mildmay was determined to win the Grand National. In the immediate post-war years that dream had every appearance of coming true. The man who, while at Cambridge, had been a moderate point-to-point rider now resumed his riding career with an authority that he had previously lacked. Young horses, chosen carefully from France and Ireland, arrived at Fairlawne and soon blossomed into winning material.

The cry of 'Come on, m'Lord' echoed all over Britain's racetracks and it often worked. As a West Countryman who was honoured to count him as a friend and was privileged to wear pale blue and white hoops on several occasions in point-to-points, I can vouch for the adoration which surrounded him, particularly in Devon and Cornwall.

There are many stories about his exploits. There was the time at his favourite racecourse, Devon and Exeter when, leading the small field two fences from home in a chase, one of the three professionals behind him shouted in an agonized voice, 'For Christ's sake, go on m'lord, we're not off!', implying that they were not trying to win!

Anthony never carried the knowledge which he had gained while riding into the Stewards' Room, which he graced with tremendous authority. He was destined to be one of the finest administrators in the history of British racing. In those days the National Hunt Committee and the Jockey Club were separate entities. Shortly before his death Anthony told me, 'They have finally persuaded me to become a member of the Jockey Club. I never wanted to be, but now that I have accepted, God help them! They're going to regret it!'

And regret it they would have, because in those days, unlike today, the Jockey Club were completely hidebound and obsessed with the power of privilege, which 'Lordy' undoubtedly was not. His greatest achievement was to bring into steeplechasing the finest patron it has ever known, Queen Elizabeth. He was Champion Amateur for five years in succession. In 1945–46 he rode eleven winners, in 1946–47 thirty-two, in 1947–48 twenty-two, in 1948–49 thirty, and in 1949–50 thirty-eight, a total which took him into fifth place in the professional ranks.

For the two years before the 1948 Grand National the public had given Anthony Mildmay growing support as he rode at big meetings and small. They remembered his hard-luck defeat on Davy Jones and respected his courageous dedication. Moreover they recognized him to be a genuine amateur, representing the best of the past in a society racked by change. His favourite horse was Cromwell, now seven years old and handicapped at 10 st 11 lb. Once again the West Country was on him to a man.

Neville watched the race with his new owner, who was constantly fortifying himself from a large flask of brandy. Prince Regent was there again, thirteen years old but still formidable. As the field circled round and then began to line up, with the nerves of the jockeys communicating themselves to the horses, Anthony Mildmay's luck began to wane. Cromwell was kicked and took a long time to recover. During the first circuit he jumped sluggishly, so far back at the water that he seemed to have no chance.

But it was a very good start – Musical Lad was the only one to suffer – and they all went away at a cracking pace, a beautiful sight in the bright sunshine. The going was on top of the ground and little Lough Conn, as usual, took up the running, with Cloncarrig outside him. The favourite, Lord Bicester's lovely class chaser Silver Fame, was brought down at Becher's, and as they turned at the Canal for the first time Johnny Hislop on Cloncarrig took up the running, with First of the Dandies, ridden by Jimmy Brogan, close up, Fulke Walwyn's Rowland Roy nicely placed and Cromwell still some way behind but beginning to warm up.

Cloncarrig pecked badly at the fence before the Chair, leaving First of the Dandies in front, where he was to stay until the last few strides. Twenty-five horses jumped the water in front of the stands, a water which was far wider than today. Away they went for the second circuit. First of the Dandies was lightly weighted with only 10 st 4 lb, and Brogan was riding with tremendous confidence as he turned into the country followed by Rowland Roy, Parthenon, Maltese Wanderer, Happy Home and Prince Regent, once more gallantly defying the years and the weight. The visibility was wonderful and as they went away down past the embankment in that third mile Cromwell was improving steadily, reaching Becher's in the leading group, apparently full of running. But several months before Anthony Mildmay had broken his neck at Folkestone, since when he had been afflicted by sudden cramp in the muscles of his neck. It had happened before during a minor race and had mattered little. It happened with a mile remaining. Unable to raise his head, he could not see more than a few yards. He could only sit motionless, chin on chest, in an attitude of despair. To those of us watching he seemed to have given up. Everyone in the crowd who knew him and indeed almost worshipped him was bewildered. Only his friends guessed and suffered with him as he rode blind, leaving it to the horse. It was a memorable piece of courage, but it could not be enough.

Gradually the number thinned until at Valentine's second time round there were only a few survivors in the race with a chance, with First of the Dandies, Sheila's Cottage, and Zahia in the first group. Neville says, 'The winner looked sure to come from one of seven runners – and Sheila's Cottage was among them on the inside. First of the Dandies, who had led over Valentine's, increased his lead as he came onto the racecourse pursued by Zahia, with our horse next.

'Then came the real drama of the race as First of the Dandies jumped the second last just ahead of Zahia. That's where the horses come from the circular course into the home straight, and everyone gasped as Zahia continued on the round course out of the race. By then I could hardly take my eyes off Sheila's Cottage as Arthur drove her relentlessly on in pursuit of First of the Dandies, who jumped the last with a useful advantage.'

Arthur says, 'I don't think Zahia would have won. First of the Dandies was about six lengths in front of me with Barry Brogan, Jimmy's son, at the last fence and I thought I hadn't a hope of catching him. He seemed to be going very easy and I was flat out. But you see things better when you are in the air and I saw First of the Dandies waver a little bit and thought to myself that that was the first sign of tiredness. It made me ride twice as hard. She was hanging like hell on the rails and I could not get her out from the wing of the last fence. I thought, Well, I can't go round him, because she's hanging too much. So I knew I would have to go right up through the inside whether I liked it or not. And that's just what happened. We were within half a length of him at the junction and I knew then that I had won the National. First of the Dandies hung on and I hated him. Brogan knew I was coming and could not stop me.'

Neville says, 'There was Sheila's Cottage eating up the ground and closing with every stride. She joined the leader 150 yards from the post, and though he was tiring and bumped her, she went by him to win by a length. We'd won the National! I could hardly believe it. Dear old Sheila's Cottage. She'd done it for me. The first mare to win the National since Shannon Lass in 1902.'

As they reached the elbow Neville had turned to his owner and said, 'Here, John, look. Don't laugh, but we might win this.' He laughs, 'And there was John Procter sitting back with a flask of brandy going glug, glug, glug. He said, "I don't want to watch the bloody National. You do your business and I'll do mine."' The prize to the winner that year was £9103. Procter had to pay his clients in the pub at 50–1!

As Neville's hat flew miles into the air, Anthony Mildmay on Cromwell finished an honourable third, only six lengths behind First of the Dandies. Zahia's jockey, Eddie Reavey, who had misunderstood the peculiarities of the run-in, possibly squandering the chance of a lifetime, was to mourn later, 'I was only cantering. I must have won, no question.' But great races are not won by hard luck stories.

My personal memory of that race was Neville bursting through the crowd round the winner's enclosure. As he smacked the winner on the rump with an endearing 'Well done, you old bitch' her lightning fast hind leg missed his head by three inches, but his splendidly happy grin never changed.

Neville says, 'After that I never looked back. Suddenly I was the wonder boy and everyone wanted me to train for them. We soon got full up in the yard, although they were all jumpers. As I said before, if I'd had some flat horses I might have had a penny or two instead of being skint!

'We went back to the Adelphi Hotel that night and, needless to say, I did not get home until the next day. Then everyone came to Warwick House and gave the horse a fabulous reception. A couple of days later a press photographer turned up to take a picture with Arthur on top. And what did she do? Sheila's Cottage bit the top off one of his fingers while he was trying to put on her bridle! I told him to go to the doctor, but he was a tough old sod. He just got up on the horse and they got their picture.'

Neville and Brownie's daughter Sarah was six years old at the time. She says, 'I did not go to that National, but I can remember listening to it on the radio. There were tremendous celebrations when they all came back to Middleham and the whole village turned out to greet them. There is a picture of me hanging on to the end of Sheila's Cottage as we came into the yard. I suppose it was a wonder I wasn't killed, but when you don't know you are usually all right. She was certainly vicious. I can still remember her biting the top off Arthur's finger!'

At that time Sarah was at her first school, going daily to a little convent at Richmond. 'It was a very religious convent,' she says. 'They had saints' days every five minutes and on these occasions we were always sent home for the day. I decided I did not want to go to school that day so I said to my friend, "Let's make up a saint's day. Mum and Dad won't know whether we have got the right day or not." So we got on the bus and went back into Leyburn and had tea at her house. We were having a lovely time when suddenly the telephone went and it was the Mother Superior. She said that they had lost my friend and Miss Crump. I overheard this and was really frightened, so I ran out of the house into the main square. I panicked and stood there with tears running down my face wondering how I could get home. A little old lady came up and bunged me into a taxi. She took me home to Warwick House. Mum had had a telephone call too and was mad with me. As she was graciously saying thank you to this old lady I shot upstairs and hid in a wardrobe. Mum said, "I don't know what your father is going to say!" Dad had gone off to Ireland buying horses and I was trembling all day, waiting for him to come home. He arrived, bouncing in, and told me that Mum had informed him that I had been terrible. "Never mind!" he said and gave me the most enormous fluffy toy dog.'

Sheila's Cottage never ran again. Even in the euphoria of the big race Neville had told the press that there was a doubt about her running because of soreness from a splint. 'But I let her take her chance. If I have my way she will never run again but go straight to stud, where I hope to have her mated with a good miler.' Neville had his way and sent her to stud immediately. She was covered by Scottish Union, Mr Jimmy Rank's St Leger winner.

The postscript to Sheila's Cottage's Grand National win is told by John Penney, now well known as a journalist, broadcaster and television commentator. John joined Neville shortly after the National as a pupil/assistant trainer, having just been demobilized from the Queen's Bays. He recalls, 'Later that year, when we were at Newcastle, some very pompous, up-stage chap asked, "Oh, Crump, have you got that mare in foal yet?" "No," said Neville, "I don't know what they are messing about at. Reckon I could do a damn sight better than that stallion if I took on the job myself."'

Like many top-class mares, who are apt to have more than their fair share of male hormones, Sheila's Cottage was not a great success at stud. She had six foals, of which only the last, Cottager, a bay gelding by Umidwar, foaled in 1960, was any good. He won a point-to-point and, trained by Fred Winter, a hurdle race and four chases.

Procter lost his money and told Neville that he was going to have the mare put down. Neville was damned if he was going to have the horse which had achieved his ambition and changed his life turned into dogs' meat, so he persuaded Procter to give her to Arthur Thompson. So Sheila's Cottage travelled back to the land of her birth and ended her days on Arthur's farm in Wexford. She is buried at the bottom of his garden.

7

In early May 1948 another of John Procter's horses, Prince Ki, who had won on the flat at the Liverpool National meeting, was due to compete in the Chester Cup. Chester is an ideal meeting. It is important for trainers to realize that a happy day out makes a lot of difference to their owners, particularly if they are disappointed by the running of their horses. The May meeting vies with Ayr's Western Meeting and the two main meetings at York and Goodwood for the most enjoyable fixture of the flat-racing season, always excluding Newmarket.

Owners can stay at Chester's well-run hotels, which are usually in gala mood, and walk down the old Tudor Rows to the delightful little amphitheatre on the outskirts of the town. The course is flat and only 1 mile 73 yards round. And it is round, just like a saucer. Left-handed, it is no place for a big, long-striding horse, but the value and prestige of the races, plus the fact that Cheshire cheeses are given to the winners at the main meeting, attract many top-class performers and classic hopes. You need a nippy horse and a jockey with guts and dash. Chester is no place for chicken-hearted riders. The tight bends soon find them out.

John Penney says, 'For Chester we used to stay just outside Liverpool, by the seaside. John Procter, was also staying at our luxury hotel. He got hold of the newsreel of the Grand National and after dinner we saw the film through. "Good old girl, she's won!" So we celebrated. "Let's put it on again. God, she's going to do it again!" We celebrated again. The film was played through time and time again, and each time Sheila's Cottage won we had to celebrate again. In the end we were watching it completely pie-eyed!

'The next morning, feeling much the worse for wear, I had to get up early and go down to the Chester track to see Prince Ki work. When I came back, who should be on the back doorstep but Crumpie and John Procter. "Come here, you great big bugger, we got your breakfast!" Champagne and boiled eggs. It was great! And then Arthur Thompson came in from the sands with a couple of donkeys which he brought into the hotel.'

Prince Ki, ridden by Harry Blackshaw, led first time round, was boxed in, caught the rails and pulled up lame. He later became a useful staying hurdler.

On one occasion, when he was running at Cheltenham, Neville was in bed with flu. He says, 'Arthur Thompson got away with murder. When he was riding Prince Ki at Cheltenham, the French jockey Bobby Bates was there – the chap who spoke English perfectly well but couldn't understand a word of it whenever he was had up in front of the Stewards. On this occasion Arthur did Bates twice in the same race. He came up on his inside and pushed him and then came up on his outside and pushed him. Bates came back to the weighing room, shouting, "Theese bloody Eengleesh! He came up my right side, he came up my outside." Arthur shouted back, "I'll come up your bloody backside if you don't shut up!"

'Colonel Squeak Thompson, who was a Steward, telephoned me to say, "You've got a right jockey there. Why don't you warn him off?" I said, "I can't. He's too nice."' And Brownie says, 'Arthur got away with murder – he was such a charmer!'

To get some idea of the dramatic influx of horses to Warwick House after Sheila's Cottage's success you have to look at the diary which John Penney kept. Before the Grand National there were only about half a dozen horses in the yard. Within a few months there were thirty and Neville was obliged to build a bottom yard. Before long even that was not enough. He had to have horses billeted in stables around the village. 'He actually had sixty-six horses at one time,' says Brownie. Neville takes her word for it but finds it hard to believe. He told

John Penney, 'No man can train a hundred horses. In my eyes sixty is about the maximum. You have a first lot of about twenty-five to thirty, a second lot of about twenty, and then about half a dozen for the third lot.'

And John adds, 'All the same, at evening stables he goes round and looks at every horse thoroughly and talks to the lads.

'He has always done a lot of office work. He is so conscientious and meticulous that he likes to do it all himself. I have sat with him on many occasions when various owners kept telephoning with big ideas and he would tell me, "Always remember, training the horse is no problem; the problem is training the owner. The other thing is, never train for bookmakers."

'I was with Neville one night when the owner of two horses, one of which was a first-class chaser, telephoned, obviously to say that his horse should be "not off" [not trying] when it ran next day. Crump really hit the ceiling. He said, "No, I've never done it and I'm never going to do it. That horse will go to the meeting and it will win. When the race is over, you will find both your horses in the racecourse stables. What you do with them then is up to you!" He slammed the telephone down, and that is exactly what happened.'

There were many good horses, both on the flat, like Keepatwoatwo and Sporting Statute, who topped the Northern Free Handicap, and over fences, such as Part Point, who won a few good chases and ran in the 1951 Grand National, Shining Gold and Sporting Link.

The list of owners includes Ivor Sainsbury, Major and Mrs Victor McCalmont, Denny and Cynthia Thompson, Alex Abraham, Captain Tom Wilson, owner of Wot No Sun, Major Arthur Straker and Lady Bache Hay.

It is Arthur Straker's son, former 11th Hussars officer, Major Ivan Straker, who, as chairman of Seagrams Distillers UK, has, with Edgar Bronfman, president of Seagram Europe, been instrumental in saving the National for posterity. Ivan, justifying Seagram's wonderful rescue operation, says, 'I thought that we as a nation could not afford to let the Grand

National die. It is part of our heritage, the greatest sporting spectacle in the whole world. It is bigger than all of us, epitomizing as it does the union between man and horse as nothing else can do. It belongs to the world and it was quite beyond me to imagine why the appeal was in danger of foundering.

'When, in 1983, I read the news that the Grand National appeal was in danger and that the end was surely in sight, I went upstairs to see Edgar Bronfman, grandson of Seagram's founder and son of the present chairman. Extraordinarily, he knew why I had come. "Yes," he said, "you can have half a million. Go ahead and save the National."

'I asked how he would tell the North American shareholders. Edgar replied, "Ivan, Britain has given my family company fifty years of unparalleled opportunity in the world of wines and spirits. In return for what they have given us I would like to give them back a bit of their heritage." In the end £400,000 was the sum required and the race was saved.'

The Strakers of Northumberland, Masters of Tynedale Foxhounds for 104 successive years, whose name epitomizes all that is best in British sport, have been associated with Aintree for more than a century. The Seagram motto – 'Tradition, craftsmanship and integrity' – might serve as the motto of the Grand National itself. And now Ivan has bought a horse to be trained by Neville, and so once more the family's famous black with lilac cap may well be carried to victory to equal the National record of four winners.

Ivan and his sister, Dawn Goodfellow, who now trains successfully in her own right, recall the long friendship between their mother and father, Arthur and Cecily and Neville and Brownie Crump. Dawn says, 'In those early days the Crump horses were turned out at our home, Pawston.'

The list of the heroes of 1948 includes Platypus, Sporting Link, Sporting Statute, Keepatwoatwo ('Keepatwat,' says Neville), Shining Gold and Wot No Sun. The following year Wot No Sun won Neville's first Scottish Grand National.

Arthur says, 'He was the bravest little horse in the world, that one. He didn't have the best of legs and three miles was really his limit.'

They were all winners and the name of Crump was already a household word. One day, soon after Sheila's Cottage had won the Grand National, Neville went to Bangor on Dee. John Penney says, 'Neville went to the owners' and trainers' entrance and the gateman asked, "Name?" "Crump, Neville Crump," Neville replied. "What do you do?" the gateman asked. "Train," said Neville. "You've never heard of me?" "Yes," the gateman said. "I've heard of Crump. But how do I know it's you?"

'Up came Bobby Renton, the well-known northern trainer "Morning, Mr Renton. Do you know this man?"

"Oh no. I don't know him from Adam." Bobby always had a sense of humour and realized that Crump was having a bit of stick from that gateman.'

In the 1949 National, won by Russian Hero, from Roimond, ridden by Dick Francis, Wot No Sun was brought down, and three out Arthur Thompson's mount, Astra, was baulked. This was the year when Monaveen first ran in the Grand National. The following year he took part again. He had been bought in the meantime for the Queen and her daughter Princess Elizabeth, the present Queen Mother and Queen, and ran in the Princess's colours. This was the first time that royal colours had been carried in the race since the death of King Edward VII in 1910.

The 1950 race represented Lord Mildmay's last attempt to achieve his life's ambition. He was now forty years old, well beyond the age when many steeplechase amateurs elect to retire, but as he prepared to ride Cromwell for the third time there was no mention of imminent retirement.

Arthur Thompson says, 'I rode Persian Pageant in a hurdle race at Liverpool on National day. I was riding pretty hard into the last hurdle and he fell. A horse came along and kicked me in the head, squashing my nose. I told the doctors that I wanted to ride in the National whatever happened and the racecourse doctor passed me fit. I don't even remember starting. I went all the way round to the Canal Turn second time before I realized it was a race.

'By then Wot No Sun was so tired that he was drunk. But he still carried on and kept jumping and finished second. Now, he was a good horse. But the poor little chap was absolutely out on his feet at the Canal Turn. God, he had a heart as big as himself!'

There had been a lot of grief on the first circuit. Anthony Mildmay's luck had struck again at the eleventh, where Cromwell had been brought down. Monaveen had made a bad mistake at the fourteenth, but was still there with a chance as the survivors galloped towards Becher's for the second time. Angel Hill, ridden by Tommy Shone, went into the lead and looked like running away with it until he hit the Canal fence. Shagreen, a strong tip before the race, fell, leaving Cloncarrig in front, followed by Freebooter. As they took the long bend from Valentine's towards the second last Cloncarrig seemed to be moving smoothly. But as Jimmy Power on Freeboother closed with him, Bob Turnell asked Cloncarrig for a further effort. The horse tried to respond but misjudged his jump, hit the fence and stood on his nose. Freebooter won from Wot No Sun and Acthon Major.

A son of Steel Point, Freebooter, a magnificent individual, had been bought as an unbroken three-year-old for 620 guineas. He then passed on for 3000 guineas to Mrs Brotherton, to be trained by Aintree specialist Bobby Renton, who saddled the winners of every steeplechase at Aintree during more than fifty years of training. When he was over seventy he still liked to ride in one race a season himself.

On 12 May 1950 Lord Mildmay left his home at Mothercombe in Devon to go down to the beach, as was customary, for a pre-breakfast swim. He was never seen alive again. Presumably he was a victim of the same sudden cramp which had deprived him of the National in 1948.

Shining Gold was a top-class 2-mile chaser. Neville says, 'Brian Marshall thought he was sure to win a Champion Hurdle, but he was no good on soft ground and finished last. But he did win us lots of two-mile chases. I bought him in

Ireland for Ivor Sainsbury for 5000 guineas, which, I suppose, was quite a lot of money in those days.

'He was a great leaper and I remember how he proved it one day at Carlisle when he overjumped a fence which was out of sight of the stands and all but came down. Two fences later he was back in the hunt and going strongly when Arthur Thompson really put him to the test. Guy Cunard's horse had refused and Guy was lying there in a heap on top of the fence. "Keep still and you'll be all right," shouted Arthur. And he was. Shining Gold sailed over them both quite easily. Guy was absolutely furious.'

Between 1949 and 1964 Neville was in the leading six on the Trainers' List no fewer than ten times. He was Champion Trainer twice, in 1951–52 and in 1956–57. He won his first Welsh Grand National with Skyreholme in 1951. He won three different Grand Nationals – Aintree, Scottish and Welsh – in three successive years. And there was more to come. In 1952 Blackpool and Shining Gold brought off a unique double when they won the Victory Hurdle and the Victory Chase at Manchester six weeks after they had done the same thing at Doncaster in the two Princess races. Lockerbie and Boned Turkey were two more of the Crump chasing stars.

The headlines at the time are quite remarkable: 'Neville Crump's Grand Team of Jumpers'; 'Crump sends three to Leicester and all win'; 'Neville Crump makes it 32'; 'Crump and Thompson make a Leicester haul'; 'Big advance in trainer's winnings'; 'Crump's seven wins in a run'; 'Everyone enjoys the Crump wins'; 'First five runners of 1952 all won.'

Some idea of the regard in which Neville was held, even in 1950 at the very beginning of his career, can be gained from the fact that he was the only jump trainer to be invited to the exclusive Gimcrack Dinner at York. The ultra-select company included the Comte de Chambure, the Comte François de Brignac and Marcel Boussac, the overlord of French racing. Also at the high table were the Earl of Scarborough, the Lord Mayor of York, the Marquis of Zetland, Lord Willoughby de Broke, Colonel Dick Warden and Lord Irwin. Neville has kept the menu, which makes fascinating reading today.

Royales Natives
Saumon Fumé d'Ecosse
—

Tortue Claire au Marsala
—

Suprême de Sole Breval
—

Jambon d'York au
Champagne
—

Faisan Rôti sur Canapé
—

Bombe Plombière Frivolités
Laitances Diablées Sur
Toast

Gimcrack
Champagne

Moet & Chandon
1943

Ch. Lafite
Pauillac

Dow's Port
1927

When she was eight years old Sarah went to school in Westmorland, at Windermere. 'In those days, when you went to school, you jolly well stayed there – none of this home every weekend or anything like that,' she says. 'I was lucky if I saw my parents once a term. I hated it. I used to cause terrible scenes. I was always running away from the school.

'One day, when I could stand it no longer, I ran up to the headmistress in the senior school and said, "I hate your school and I hate everybody here!" Right in the middle of lunch that was. I had a photograph of Warwick House and Mum and Dad and said, "And that's my Mummy and Daddy and I want to go home."'

At home Sarah went racing as often as she could and in the evening would try to go to the cinema. 'We had a terrible little flea pit in Middleham where all the stable lads used to go. Mum was not too keen for me to go there, but it was the only form of entertainment that there was in the village. I used to ask Mum if I could go to the pictures and she always said

106

"No." And I would go and ask Daddy, knowing full well that I could get round him. He would let me out of the window and I would jump down into the street. He was marvellous.

'Dad has always adored his dogs. And so has Mum. As a family we are tremendously dog-minded. At about this time I had a whippet and Mum had a Dalmatian bitch called Mitzie who had a litter. My whippet was run over, and as we had the puppies at the time Mum immediately made me come down to choose one for myself. She kept one and I had one. We had those two sisters for ages.

'Then there was the time when a bitch died having puppies. We had all these dear little things on our hands. So Dad telephoned a place where you could get a bitch with some milk as a foster mother. We ended up with this dear old dog who was supposed to stay with us for only as long it took to rear the pups. But Dad just could not bear to send her back. So he telephoned the owner who said we could not have her. The poor old dog was a Lassie-type sheep dog of about twelve years old. Dad insisted that he would not let her go and so the man charged him the most monumental amount. He got his money and we had her for quite a long time. Dad has always been like that with dogs.'

Part of the secret for Neville's phenomenal success is that he not only loves animals but understands them. Brownie says, 'He hunted whenever he had the chance and he had one particularly good hunter, a fine big horse. But if you were by yourself and wanted to get him back into the trailer he was a real sod. One day Neville was coming back from hunting and there was not a soul about. This bloody horse would not go into the trailer and Neville nearly went mad. So in the end he thought, Right! If you want to stay out, you can stay out! So he shut the back of the trailer, tied the horse on behind, got in and drove off! This old horse was clip-clopping behind!'

Neville says, 'It was a very small road and someone stopped me and said, "Do you know you've got a horse behind?" and I said, "Yes, I do. And the bastard is going to stop there for another two miles." So when I got to the other end I opened the door and he went straight in!'

Brownie laughs. 'The head man we had at that time used to feed a common horse the same way as you would feed a racehorse. Of course, they don't need the same amount of oats. One morning Neville got up on this big horse and the damn thing carted him straight up the churchyard! Neville got him round and then he went full gallop up the street. You can imagine the language that was flying!'

Flat or jumping Birmingham was a wonderful racecourse. It was a real professionals' track, scrupulously fair under both rules. It had a straight flat course, the draw made no difference, and a novice jumper had plenty of time to get round the bend and see his fence or hurdle before he faced up to it. Moreover you saddled in your boxes by the paddock. Its loss was a real tragedy for the sport. Now that wonderful course is forgotten, obliterated under Spaghetti Junction.

Neville says, 'One day I was driving to Birmingham and was stopped for speeding. The policeman said "Are you in a hurry?" I said, "Yes. I've got one in the first race." He said, "Will it win?" "Yes," I said. "If I get there in time to declare it!" So he let me go and I looked out of my rear-view mirror and saw him running into a telephone box. The horse won all right.'

8

Teal was a nicely turned bay gelding by Bimco out of Miltown Queen. He was bred in Tipperary by Gerald Carroll, who had considerable difficulty selling him. 'Gerald couldn't get a fiver for him as a two-year-old,' says Neville.

Thumbing through the archives, I came across corroboration of the Teal story from the late Clive Graham, then the Scout of the *Daily Express*, and his colleague, Peter O'Sullevan. They wrote in 1952: 'It hardly seems credible that eight years ago Teal, then a two-year-old, was on offer for £5. His breeder, Gerald Carroll, of Co. Tipperary, confirmed, "Two prospective buyers refused the horse at this price."' Eventually a bargain was struck with Dick Gough, a Tipperary neighbour: £35 changed hands for Teal and another horse.

There was nothing striking about Teal's appearance or pedigree, and at that time his future was visualized as just another inmate of a hunting or riding stable. He was put up for auction at Stockton Sales and bought by Mr Patterson for 32 guineas. Binco, as Teal was called at this time, because he was by Bimco, found little favour with the different Yorkshire owners whose property he became during the next four years.

As a six-year-old he was repurchased by Mr Patterson and lent to a neighbouring farmer, Mr Laurence Gibson, for his daughter to ride. Miss Joan Gibson found the headstrong Binco too much of a handful – in fact the horse spent several hours during 1948 careering solo round the Yorkshire moors. So he was sent to Mr Ridley Lamb of Ingleby, Berwick, in exchange for another horse, and started to win a few point-to-points.

Arthur Thompson recalls, 'It was at Hexham at the end of the season that I noticed this little horse lengths in front at halfway. Thereabouts he fell, or his jockey might have come off. The chap was sitting on the floor and the horse was standing beside him, looking at him. He must have been a bit shaken because he didn't get up straightaway. All the horses had gone past and were three or four fences ahead of them by now. When he eventually got back on he had about half a mile to make up. Believe me, Teal was in front after the last fence and only just got beat.

'I saw Harry Lane there and told him that if he wanted to win the National he should buy the horse. He bought him from Ridley for £3000 and sent him to Neville Crump.'

Neville has always been a great believer in Atty Persse's oft-stated theory: 'A jumping trainer means a man who trains his horses to jump. If they fall, you are falling down on your job.' Like the late Fred Rimell, joint holder with the Hon. Aubrey Hastings of the Grand National record of four winners, Neville has tremendous faith in the loose school which he built at Middleham. All the young horses are put in the loose school where they soon find their bearings and get accustomed to being enclosed before they jump over fixed obstacles completely loose. The horses soon come to love it and you have to stop them jumping round and round. The great benefit of the loose school is that the horse makes its own mistakes and learns how to put itself right. It discovers the most natural way to jump properly and acquires a sense of timing which it is unlikely ever to lose. Then, ridden, they were schooled steadily over the schooling fences at Low Moor.

Arthur says, 'One of the reasons why Neville is such a wonderful trainer is that he has never left anything undone. Everything has to be seen to. I think horses can be over-schooled. Never overschool them or school too fast. They have to learn to use themselves when they are jumping. There is an awful lot to handling horses. You see jockeys cracking whips and walloping the horses and it only upsets them. You have to treat them kindly and they'll treat you kindly. Neville and I were never rough on horses. But, like him, my one thought when I went out on a horse was to win. No matter what it was, I was dead bent on winning.'

So, back to Teal and his big, heavy-betting owner, who

made Neville and Arthur stop a horse for the only time in their respective lives.

'Anyway, we schooled Teal over a few fences before we ran him and his first race was at Kelso, over 2½ miles.'

Kelso is a charming little left-handed jumping course with two separate tracks. For hurdles, an oval circuit of 1 mile 1½ furlongs; for chasing, a rectangular track of 1¼ miles and 160 yards. This has a long run-in of a quarter of a mile – too long, perhaps, because this puts too large a premium on speed and less on jumping. However, it also calls for a fair degree of stamina. Northern trainers regard Kelso highly and frequently run some of their best chasers here in preparation for big events.

For Kelso races the Crump horses used in those days to be stabled at Floors Castle, home of the Duke of Roxburghe, a large, florid Jockey Club member who still believed in the divine right of peers.

Neville had already told Harry Lane that Teal was a very good horse. He had worked him with Shining Gold on Wetherby racecourse, giving lumps of weight away. Teal won the gallop easily. So Harry Lane was determined to have an enormous bet on his horse in the Grand National. But on the occasion that Teal ran for the first time at Kelso he had not yet backed the horse.

Before the race Neville was summoned to the telephone in the weighing room. It was Harry Lane. In a belligerent tone he said, 'I'm going to have a big bet on this horse for the National, and if you win with it today, I swear to you, he'll leave your yard first thing.'

Outraged, Neville replied, 'I'm not going to stop any bloody horse for you. I have never stopped one in my life and I'm not going to start now.'

Lane shouted back, 'Well, if you don't stop him today, I promise you, he'll leave your yard first thing in the morning, and that's flat.' Everyone could hear him.

Neville was bewildered and upset. For him, Captain Neville Crump, to stop a horse was unthinkable. Yet he loved Teal and knew how good he was. It was equally unthinkable for him to lose this great racehorse. In agitation he explained his predicament to Arthur Thompson, ending with, 'Look, we'd better not win today.' Arthur was flabbergasted. Like Neville, he had never stopped a horse in his life. In the end it was the intelligence and ingenuity of this remarkable jockey that saved the day.

Arthur says, 'Teal was going so fast and so low over the fences that he was actually hurting my feet. If anything, after that, he picked up and never touched anything again. But now I was so far in front, leading them a pretty dance. I was a fence in front at halfway when I pulled Teal up. I dismounted and picked up his foot, thinking that if there were any inquiries I could say that I thought he must have got a stone in his foot because he was going lame. When the other horses passed me, I jumped up again and we still finished second. That was the only way I could have stopped him, on the far side of the course where few could see what was happening. It just shows what a remarkable horse he was to finish second under those circumstances.'

Bill Smith, who looked after Teal all the time he was with Neville, remembers 'Bobo' Roxburghe coming into the box and saying angrily to Neville, 'Don't do that again, Neville, or you'll get warned off.' For once Roxburghe was right. But Neville didn't like being told off in front of the other Stewards and to defuse the situation he made a joke of it. 'Do you know what Bobo says? He says I stopped that horse!' Fortunately, the other Stewards laughed at the very idea of Neville pulling up a horse and nothing came of it.

Arthur continues Teal's story. 'Then we ran at Cheltenham, where there were about twenty-four of us in a three-mile chase. I thought I would just see what Teal could do. It was very heavy ground. I was thinking about the Kelso race and set off in front, thinking he was sure to stop, but the farther we went the faster he was going. I let him go right from the beginning. The trouble was that he kept getting so far in front. It happened so easily. When I got to the top of the hill I thought there was no one else in the race so I started to ease him down. The only mistake he made was at the last. He never looked like falling but he made a hash of it because we were going too slowly.'

Now that Harry Lane had made his enormous bet at 33–1 for the Grand National, the preparation went on. Arthur says, 'We ran him at Newbury where he put his foot in a hole at the ditch in the straight first time round and fell. That was the only time he did fall properly. Then we took him to Birmingham the following week and I could not pull him up after the race, which was four miles. He dropped from 50–1 that day to 100–8.'

That Birmingham Handicap Chase was the most extraordinary affair in which Teal and Pearly Prince had a thrilling duel. Up to the last fence there was never more than a length between them, Pearly Prince keeping up with Teal by virtue of his wonderful jumping. This always gave him a slight advantage, well as Teal flew the fences at his side.

It was a wonderful race to watch. Teal and Pearly Prince, who was receiving 9 lb from his rival, set a cracking pace from the start. Before they had gone a mile all except Teal, Pearly Prince, Galloway Braes, who was later to become one of the top chasers of his generation, and Mountain Earl had gone out with the washing.

Galloway Braes, who had run out when leading his field in the Grand International at Sandown a short while before, moved up close behind the two leaders at halfway and was travelling very well when he disappeared from view in a cloud of spray at the water jump second time round. By now no one else, except for the mare Elseena, was even remotely in touch. She only got up close behind the two leaders turning up the straight. She was apparently going very well when she fell at the last fence. It was then, on the flat, that Teal pulled out a little more speed, which Pearly Prince could not match, and ran out a really good winner by four lengths in a time of 7 minutes 1/5 second.

So the scene was set for the Grand National. It is difficult to remember the mystique which surrounded Neville Crump and Arthur Thompson at that time. Both were regarded as the very greatest in their profession. Not long before Aintree, the late

Claud Harrison wrote an article headed 'The Trainer with a Problem'. It ran:

> You might call Neville Crump the trainer with a problem. He has four horses in the Grand National, Teal, Wot No Sun, Traveller's Pride and Skyreholme, and all have their different claims. Even the stable opinions are divided.
>
> 'If I could ride one of them it would be Skyreholme,' was the trainer's opinion. 'He stays well and jumps well. He has had a "leg", but I believe it is all right now and if he stays sound I shall fancy him very much.'
>
> Skyreholme won the Welsh Grand National for Neville over 3¾ miles last season and should not be troubled by the extra six furlongs at Aintree.
>
> Earlier I had called on jockey Arthur Thompson and discussed the prospect of his National mount, Teal (on which he won the Birmingham Handicap Steeplechase yesterday).
>
> Said Arthur, 'I think he is a really good horse, a bold and accurate jumper, just the sort to get round Aintree. I feel confident he will stay the journey.'
>
> When I mildly chided him for turning down my favourite, Wot No Sun, he admitted he did so with regret.
>
> The trainer's opinion of Teal is equally high, but he added that the only thing against him is that he may be thought a bit 'novicey' and 'green' compared with some of those he will be meeting.
>
> Before falling at Newbury in December, the horse had won his two previous races without the semblance of a mistake, one over 3 miles at Cheltenham. So it is Tea for Two – Teal and Thompson.
>
> Of Wot No Sun, Captain Crump had this to say, 'He is a great jumper and seems completely sound again. He must have a very fair chance on all his running and his second of two years ago when Arthur Thompson rode him. I am delighted with him.'

The previous year, 1951, the Grand National had suffered a severe setback. The starter had pressed his lever while many of the horses were still walking around. Jockeys were adjusting their caps and their reins. Some were checking their girths. Suddenly they heard the rattle of the tape and an incredulous wail went up from the stands. They turned their horses as best as they could and set off in pursuit. The previous year's winner, Freebooter, was among them.

There seemed to be no provision for recall, no attempt to rectify the most ghastly mistake in the history of the race. Owners who had spent considerable sums preparing their horses, trainers who had spent months, thousands who had travelled long distances – all were united in a roar of protest which sounded like disgust. Fiasco inevitably became tragedy at the first fence. Twelve horses came down or were brought down. The melee was without precedent. Jockeys made themselves as small as pheasants in long grass, waiting for danger to pass. Horses floundered and struggled up, looking for a way out. In effect the race ended there. During those few minutes something happened to the prestige of the Grand National from which it is only just recovering today. In the end only two were left. Nickel Coin defeated Royal Tan and the remounted Derrinstown finished third.

In 1952, although the race was to be worthy of the greatest traditions of the Grand National, there was fiasco of another kind. The Aintree executive and the BBC were involved in a dispute over copyright. The deadlock could not be resolved and the Topham administration substituted its own broadcast for the highly efficient commentary which the BBC had relayed since 1927. Half an hour before the race poor Mrs Mirabel Topham, who ran Aintree for so many years, had to make an alteration to her team of private broadcasters. One of the commentators failed to arrive and a friend of Mrs Topham who was watching the race from the County Stand agreed to do the commentary from the twelfth fence. We had the extraordinary result of what was sometimes known in the Army as a 'COMFU' – a completely organized military fuck-up! Legal Joy, a very good horse owned by the Hon. Dorothy Paget and trained by Fulke Walwyn, was described by a commentator with great gusto as 'Legal Paget'!

Nevertheless, this was one of the great Grand Nationals, run in near record time, even though the going was a little on the soft side. Harry Lane chartered a private train to bring his wife, five daughters and six hundred employees from his building/engineering works to the course. I do not believe that any jockey has ever been as confident of winning the world's toughest and greatest steeplechase as Arthur Thompson was that day when he went out telling his colleagues in the changing room that they might as well have stayed at home. One of the worst features of Aintree has always been that the main fences – Becher's and the Canal Turn – are a mile away from the stands. On a misty day it is extraordinary to see the world's press, who have travelled thousands of miles to watch this great sporting event, standing with their backs to the race, watching the television set in the back of the press box.

Neville saddled three runners – Traveller's Pride did not run. As with Sheila's Cottage four years earlier, Neville was putting his trust in a novice horse. Teal had run only five times previously in this, his first season's steeplechasing, winning three times and falling once at Newbury. It was, indeed, a remarkable performance for a virtual novice to contest the Blue Riband of steeplechasing. And, do not forget, Arthur Thompson, who was then the idol of the jumping crowds, had chosen Teal in preference to Wot No Sun or Skyreholme. Colonel Tom Nickalls described him at the time as 'the finest rider I have ever seen over this particular course, with a wonderful way of imparting his own confidence to his mounts.'

As the runners paraded and cantered down to the start, the train which Harry Lane had chartered to bring his employees to Aintree stood outside the station boldly labelled 'The Harry Lane Special – Good Luck to Teal'.

The start is just to the right of the stand at Aintree and, despite the mist over the rest of the course, we could at least see that. Remembering the previous year's fiasco, we were all a little shattered when Another Delight, Printer's Pie and Teal went through the single-strand tape in a breakaway, which held up the start for eleven minutes. Bryan Marshall dismounted from Freebooter to spare him the burden of 12 st 11 lb for as long as possible. Bobby Renton had done a remarkable job with Mrs Brotherton's top weight in the limited time at his command.

At last, in the murk which blew over the course from the Liverpool direction, the forty-seven runners were aligned again – and away. All the expected horses were prominent as they raced away for that first fence, that long run towards the first of those obstacles which look so different from any other fences in the world. Covered in gorse, they are enough to make any horse refuse unless he has the character and guts. Arthur Thompson, never one to hold back, had Teal up with Freebooter, Wot No Sun, ridden by Dave Dick, a young, swashbuckling jockey known to his friends as the Stewart Granger of the changing room, and Roimond.

We could dimly distinguish a succession of falls – the black and white of Russian Hero, winner in 1949, and the blue and yellow quartered Rank colours on Early Mist, who was to triumph for Vincent O'Brien next year. It was so misty that the colours could no longer be picked out as they went to the second fence, where Teal and Freebooter took the lead.

As long as Teal jumped the first, Arthur knew he would be all right and that they would undoubtedly win the National. He did, in fact, jump that first fence rather badly, but scrambled through and, with Arthur's strong control, picked up and never made another mistake until Becher's Brook second time round. Nevertheless Dave Dick, who was following close behind him, said that Teal skidded for twenty yards on his belly at Becher's, and that only Arthur's superb balance and horsemanship enabled the partnership to survive. Neville says that Teal gave them both an almighty scare at Becher's second time, when the horse hit the big drop fence like a tank, the impact sending them skidding the length of a cricket pitch. With Arthur sitting there like a mounted policeman, Teal struggled to his feet but went down again before the recovery was completed. By the Canal Turn they were in front again.

However, before this we had seen something that we had never imagined before. Just as Teal was racing into the enormous Chair fence, Arthur looked like being hampered by the riderless grey, Caesar's Wife, dangerously galloping up on his inside. With only one hand on the reins, he calmly caught hold of those of the loose horse and yanked her away well clear of Teal, who then jumped the big open ditch as well as any in the race.

Arthur recalls that he went to the front soon after the second fence and was always first or second with Freebooter most of the rest of the way. 'The mistake at Becher's second time round cost me the lead,' he says. 'But I was up with Freebooter jumping the Canal Turn where he fell, directly after which Legal Joy came up inside me and just led at Valentine's. From there to the last we disputed the lead and, though he may have been a little ahead over the last two fences, I knew all the way from the last open ditch [the fourth fence out] that Teal could go on and beat Legal Joy any time I chose to ask him. I let him stay there on sufferance.' Arthur adds, 'I know it sounds boastful to say, as I did before the race, that Teal was sure to win bar interference, but he was so brilliant and had such brains that I was confident he would jump the course.'

We saw on the newsreel films how splendidly Teal and Legal Joy jumped over Valentine's and over the last open ditch. They raced neck and neck down the long stretch to the second last. Wot No Sun was lagging behind, but suddenly an Irish cheer went up for Royal Tan. 'Phonsie' O'Brien had brought him up with a terrific spurt and he was only five lengths behind as Teal and Legal Joy raced together at the last jump. But this fence again proved fatal and the Irish cheers died away as Royal Tan and his rider rolled on the grass.

The duel between Teal and Legal Joy now entered its bitterest moment. Michael Scudamore, who was to win the National seven years later on Oxo, was able to keep his position on the inside at the Elbow, but Dorothy Paget's little horse could not withstand his rival's final victorious rush. It had been a desperately close thing – much closer than the final margin implied. It was a great race and an outstanding triumph for Arthur and Neville. Wot No Sun came third.

Today Arthur says, 'Teal was such a good jumper. He always placed himself. I could go to the front and keep out of trouble. The only bit of trouble I had was at the Chair when that loose horse came up beside me and looked like pushing me out. But she was near enough for me to grab at the reins and I jerked her back out of the way.

'It was actually at the fence before the Canal Turn that

Freebooter fell. Bryan Marshall may reckon that I had made Freebooter fall by shouting and yelling at him but in fact we were going hell for leather at that fence to get on the inside for the turn. Everyone thought that I'd done something to frighten Freebooter because once at Haydock I did do something to him. I was riding Wot No Sun and Tim Molony was riding Freebooter, who was only cantering around, whereas my little horse was flat out. Don't forget, my chap never went more than three miles really. It was just his heart that kept him going. It was a three and a half mile chase and over the last fence Freebooter went about three parts of a length in front of me. I suddenly remembered that one day Tim had said he couldn't move on Freebooter or disturb him in any way. So I pulled out my shillelagh and cracked him on his backside as hard as I could. I have never seen him jump better in his life!

'Of course I didn't do anything to Freebooter this time. He just stood off too far. You couldn't take chances with those Aintree fences at that time. I think they are a bit softer now.'

It was a fabulous triumph and a record-breaking day for British sport. England beat Scotland at soccer at Hampden Park; Arsenal drew with Chelsea in the semifinal of the FA Cup; England beat France 3−0 in the amateur international at Norwich; England beat Scotland 1−0 in the schools international at Wembley; and in the rugby international at Paris England beat France by 6 points to 3.

Harry Lane, who had won a six-figure sum in bets, threw his hat into the air and played football with it round the winner's enclosure. Bill Smith admits to receiving 'two grand' from him as a present − 'don't tell the Guv'nor!'

Neville's daughter Sarah was only ten years old, but she went to the National. 'It was pretty horrendous,' she says. 'I was pinned at the front of the trainers' stand, and when Teal won Mum and Dad took off. I tried to go with them but I got lost in the crowd and screamed and screamed until a great big policeman came along and put me on his shoulder. He asked me my name and I shouted, "We've won the National!" So he managed to get me to the winner's enclosure where I was handed over like a parcel and plonked in the middle of the enclosure by Dad.

'Then we went to a supper do at the Adelphi Hotel. We had dinner in the evening which Mum said that I could go to. But after coffee, in all the tremendous celebrations, Arthur Thompson decided to throw flowers at Tim Hamey. Unhappily he didn't realize that they were in a glass container, which hit Tim on the head. There was blood all over the place. That did me and I had to go to bed!

'The next day Arthur, who must have been suffering from the most monumental hangover, came along saying, "Sarah, Sarah, you will never forgive me. I am so sorry!" I adored Arthur. He was always super to me. We used to go racing and I would get so bored travelling as a little girl, but even after crashing falls he would always sit and play with me on the way home. He never got cross with me. He was so good like that.'

As Neville says, 'That was quite a day!'

In retrospect, Arthur contradicts one part of the official story. 'I missed the false start when one horse broke through the tapes and a few of them got away. I was hanging back to rest Teal. When we did get away, I was well out in front. After I got over the first few fences I knew I was going to win.'

And perhaps the most dispassionate comment came from the *Daily Telegraph* under the headline 'Cavalry National'.

A notable feature of Saturday's Grand National was that the first three to finish were trained by former Cavalry soldiers. Captain Neville Crump, trainer of the winner and of the third, was formerly in the 4th Hussars ... Mr Churchill's old regiment. It was a coincidence that, in the race after the National, Mr Churchill's Pol Roger dead-heated with Lord Rosebery's Lugana. Mr Fulke Walwyn, who had trained the National runner-up, was in the 9th Lancers. He left the regiment to go in for race riding and rode Reynoldstown to victory the following year. Captain Crump was also a good race rider and won a large number of point-to-points in pre-war days.

Today Neville says, 'Arthur always reckoned that Teal was the best horse he had ridden. They made a great team, but in the National you always need an element of luck and Arthur

Merryman II (Gerry Scott) is led into the winner's enclosure after the 1960 Grand National by his owner, Miss Winifred Wallace, with Neville beside her

Merryman II, after victory in the Scottish Grand National. Miss Winifred Wallace leads him in accompanied by Neville and Sarah

'Possibly the best horse I ever trained' – Ballylord, ridden by C. Hawkins

Sarah with a goat and Rocks Cross – the picture that inspired the poem: 'You can keep the bloody goat!'

Neville with his son-in-law Roger Walker and baby granddaughter Mandy, now grown up

Frederick and Edith, Roger and Sarah, Brownie and Neville at Sarah's wedding

Rough Tweed (D. Nicholson) leads Springbok (G. Scott) at the last fence in the 1962 Hennessy Gold Cup, but Springbok got up on the line to beat Rough Tweed by a head. Both horses were trained by Neville

Low Moor in the sixties – the trainer with his Dalmatians

'On this one the "jockey" does not fall off. He cannot get on again if he does so!' The guv'nor on his hunter

Neville flanked by the late John Christian, Senior Stewards' Secretary NH, with his first winner for Lord Cadogan, Verona Forest

Still going strong – Imperial Black (trained by Neville, with a sheepskin noseband) finished sixth in the 1984 Grand National

Above and below: Neville at his Warwick House stables at Middleham

Gerry Scott with Merryman's portrait against a background of his and Neville's triumphs

had his share. He put it down to a good-luck charm, a little cross that his sister in Ireland sent him – he kept it in his breeches and he never went round Liverpool without it.'

The following season Teal ran a great race to finish second to Vincent O'Brien's crack chaser, Knock Hard, in the Great Yorkshire Chase, the one big race which Neville has never won and yet would so dearly love to have added to his tally. In the Gold Cup Teal made a bad mistake and was obviously not quite right. He was tremendously fancied for a repeat of his Grand National triumph, and so the news that the favourite had been scratched caused a minor sensation and a startling turn-round in the betting on the race. Few bookmakers were prepared to quote any odds at all.

It was initially thought that Teal had probably injured himself at the water jump in the Gold Cup, but his owner, Harry Lane, revealed, 'I have had Teal examined five times since then. Veterinary surgeons now agree that he has a ruptured bowel.'

The day after the operation it was reported:

Teal was operated on yesterday for a ruptured bowel, but it will not be known whether it was successful for at least a week. The operation, which was a most unusual one on a horse, was performed in a specially equipped theatre in Thirsk, Yorkshire. Teal was given a general anaesthetic and is now having normal post-operative treatment, including streptomycin and penicillin injections. Great interest has been aroused in the veterinary world by the operation.

It was all to no avail. Teal died.

9

It is testimony to Neville Crump that he has had only six first jockeys riding for him since the war and all of them, with the obvious exception of his current number one, Colin Hawkins, stayed with him until they retired. Indeed, in retrospect, Arthur Thompson, who was never out of the headlines from the first time he rode for Warwick House, and whose name became a legend coupled with that of Crump, must have been one of the greatest jump jockeys the sport has ever known. He was a marvellous natural horseman, with a many good stories.

Arthur remembers well a day at Southwell. 'I was riding a terribly awkward horse called Electric Whiskers. It was impossible to keep this animal going straight. He always ran out to the right. Bryan Marshall was behind me coming up on my inside, pushing my horse out more and more. So I just reached out and pulled his bridle off, handed it to him and said, "Yours, I think!" I've never seen anyone so surprised!'

Arthur was never Champion Jockey, but he was always in the running, and it was he, of course, who in that 1952 season helped Neville to his stable total of forty-nine wins, which made him Champion Trainer for the first time.

It was in that same season that Blackpool and Shining Gold brought off their unique double of the two Princess races at Doncaster and the Victory Hurdle and the Victory Chase at Manchester. And Keepatwoatwo, who held the 5-furlong record at Thirsk, scored a hat-trick over hurdles, and Lockerbie, who had looked like winning the previous season's Cheltenham Gold Cup before he ran out of petrol on the run to the last, was also a principal contributor to the stable's total.

'Blackpool was a good horse. He was the most extraordinary character. We couldn't break him. When he came to us he was a mad thing. But I thought he was a splendid little horse and he was. Arthur and I worked on him and he became a bloody good horse. He had funny ideas. We never really tamed him and Arthur had the most awful luck. The horse won a few nice chases and then gave him the most bloody awful fall, crucifying him over a fence at Newcastle. He belonged to a funny old chap called Herbert Radcliffe, who owned a book-shop in Blackpool.'

Today, thirty years on, although Neville's enthusiasm is as great as ever, the days have long since passed when it was merely a matter of Arthur Thompson adopting his usual tactics of jumping off in front and making all. Neville says, 'That's the best way to win races if you can, but you've got to have the horses and most of mine now are not good enough for that.'

Arthur says, 'The most remarkable thing was that it didn't matter to me about front running although everyone thought that this was the way I rode. It was just the type of animal that we had, as the Captain says. You couldn't stop Shining Gold. He was a very fast, brilliant horse. I tried holding up Wot No Sun a few times and he wasn't half as good a horse that way. He was a much better horse in front. Lockerbie you couldn't even hold going down to the start!

'I think there's an awful lot to handling horses. The good horses I rode for Crump were all horses I really liked and they were good to me. Horses like Preoccupation, Sporting Link, Shining Gold and so on.

'I always seemed to fall at the wrong time, usually at the beginning of the year. I never went for X-rays. When I eventually did have one after a fall they found seven lines on my scalp from previous fractures!'

I asked Arthur why he decided to retire. 'Well, I'd had a long innings. Longer than most I think. By the end of 1956 I was forty years old. I wouldn't have given it up then, only when I was driving to the meetings I couldn't place where the car in front of me was. It seemed to be moving backwards and forwards.

'I wondered about training, but I had heart trouble and the

doctors told me that I'd have to give up the horses or give up myself. I've had a wonderful life and I was very lucky to meet Neville. He would stand by you no matter what. He would never let you down.'

It was with great reluctance that I left Arthur Thompson on his farm in County Wexford with his wife Enid, his daughter Shirley and his grandchildren. Arthur has now recovered from his illness and is back to his old self, in tremendous form. Neville telephones him frequently. There are five years between them and they remain, as they have always been, the greatest of friends. Neville says, 'You could never get away with some of the things that Arthur used to do today. He was a wonderful jockey, who was always trying to win, but he could be a real rascal!'

As a parting shot, with a reminiscent chuckle, a twinkle in the eyes of the still handsome face, Arthur said, 'If your horse is not going too well and the one upsides is going that little bit better, there's one unfailing thing to do. Just get half a length in front of him and make your horse change legs. It's amazing how it puts the other chap off his stride!'

When Arthur Thompson retired in 1956 he was succeeded as stable jockey to Warwick House by Johnny East, who had served his apprenticeship with that famous Yorkshireman, Sam Armstrong, who was soon to become the father-in-law of Lester Piggott. Johnny, too, has his share of stories.

In *The Directory of the Turf*, the *Who's Who* of the bloodstock world, Neville lists Haydock as his favourite racecourse. As we have seen, his life is governed by his absolute certainty of right and wrong. He will stop at nothing to ensure that justice, as he sees it, is done, and he will not countenance avoidable errors at any time. In an admirable profile for *Sporting Life* in 1953 James Lambie wrote: 'In his prime his 90-decibel delivery of expletives could strip the paint off the back of the stands.' Even now – though mellowed by seventy-two summers – Neville is capable of verbally crucifying anyone who has incurred his displeasure.'

James goes on to tell the story, of which Neville is himself quite fond, of the time that Neville ran D. Stanhopes dual

Topham Chase winner Roughan and Lady Hay's useful Goosander, at Haydock.

Both horses were expected to win, but, although a brilliant jumper, Roughan was, in his trainer's own words, 'the most horrible old sod: you daren't hit him otherwise he'd stop, turn round and look at you' – which is exactly what happened when the unfortunate Johnny East applied the stick at Haydock.

Crump's rage knew no bounds. No sooner had East dismounted and begun to unsaddle the beaten favourite than the trainer pushed him aside and, against all the Rules of racing, did the job himself, flinging tack all round the unsaddling enclosure in a blind fury.

The hapless East had to run about picking up the pieces before making for the sanctuary of the weighing room as Crump, in a final despairing gesture of anger and frustration, tore off his gloves and hurled them at his horse as it was being led away.

But, however fierce his outbursts are, it is well known that Crump never bears malice against anyone. Once it is out of his system, the slate is wiped clean and everything is forgotten. So it was typical that an hour after the Roughan explosion had rocked the stands, all was sweetness and light after Johnny East had won on Goosander.

As the 'horses away' signal was given, Lady Hay, who had weathered the initial tempest with refined dignity, turned to her trainer and smiled sweetly, 'Please don't throw your gloves at him, Neville, he ran such a good race.'

Johnny goes on to counter this story with another typical one of the Captain. 'On other occasions when jockeys have come back expecting the sky to fall in on them after some disaster they have found the trainer has accepted the situation philosophically. Dennis Atkins well remembers the day when the Mackeson winner Cancello started odds-on to win a four-horse race at Cheltenham.

'"The Captain didn't give me any orders," he relates, "all he said to me as I went up was 'Be careful not to get brought down.' I did get brought down at the second fence.

'"A lot of trainers would have blown their top. But all he said to me when I got back was 'That's racing'." It's the quality of the man not only as a trainer but as a person. He can take his defeats as well as he takes success.'

At the end of the 1957 season I gave up training and joined the ranks of the journalists, first with *Horse and Hound*, which still remains the happiest paper with which I have ever been associated, and then for the *Daily Mail*, whose chief racing correspondent I was shortly to become. So now I was looking at the racing scene from the outside. I soon realized that, in Gerry Scott, Neville had a natural home-bred successor to the great Arthur Thompson. A superb natural horseman with a character of shining gold like his mentor and guide Arthur, Gerry suited the Captain ideally and they forged a lasting friendship.

Gerry, who started at Warwick House as a sixteen-year-old apprentice and rode for the stable for eighteen years, describes his former guv'nor as being 'so loyal it's almost frightening. When I was still a kid, apprenticed to the Captain, I won a race for the stable on a horse that was a bit of a swine. He was really ungenuine. He never ran the same race twice. I was given the ride again the next time that he ran, which was at Haydock, but as Catterick Bridge was also on that day the Captain had to go there.

'Anyway, my horse was beaten and I finished fourth. A few days later the Captain called me to his office. If ever he wanted to talk to us or if ever we wanted to talk to him he would say, "Come and see me in the office after work." This time as I climbed upstairs to the office after morning stables I was worried stiff. It usually meant trouble, and when I got there, my worst fears were confirmed. He handed me a letter from the horse's owner. There were three foolscap pages describing the race in detail as the owner had seen it, and ending by accusing me of stopping the horse. You can imagine how I felt. I was a 7-lb-claiming apprentice who hadn't been in the yard that long and who certainly didn't expect his word to be taken against that of an owner. I was terrified.

'The Captain said, "Well, Gerry, what do you think of that?" I couldn't speak because I was terrified and I didn't know what the hell to say. But all the Captain said was, "Don't worry about it. I've told the owner that if his horse is not out of the yard by Monday, it will be out on the street on Tuesday." That's how loyal he was to every one of us and to his horses. As it happens the animal went to George Owen and never won a race!'

Gerry says that he owes a lot to Arthur Thompson. 'Arthur was wonderful to me all the time when I was an apprentice. He taught me everything.'

He also has great admiration for his predecessor, Johnny East. 'The first time I have ever seen anyone really stand up to the Captain was when Johnny did it,' he says. 'I was astonished that he should do so. We have a ploughed canter down the bottom of the fields and the ground was very bad so that all sorts of things were happening on this canter and the Captain was liable to get very excited. One morning all his best horses were going in all directions and Johnny East was riding a very expensive former French horse called Kwannin. For some reason the Captain blew Johnny up and Johnny, who obviously never really grasped that the Captain's bark is so much worse than his bite, just jumped off his horse, walked up to the Captain, said, "Here," gave Kwannin to him and walked off. I had never seen anyone do that to the Captain before.'

At home in Middleham Neville lived his life in the same direct, forthright manner as ever. He devoted his thoughts to his family, his staff and his horses. He would ride out first lot, and when possible, second lot, every day, leading the string on his hack, followed by whatever adoring dogs he had at the time.

There is no doubt that in the depth of winter Middleham Moor can be hell on earth, but even on the days when frost and blizzards turn the horses into ghostly grey shadows Neville even today will scorn the comfort and convenience of a car. One of his secrets is that, unlike many other trainers, but like any good cavalry officer, he has never been guilty of asking any of his lads to do something that he himself would not do and, for this reason, has always achieved a camaraderie with them which no car-bound trainer could ever hope to approach.

His punctuality is uncanny. His neighbours set their watches by him. He works off the hour and half hour and it is as if the clock above Kingsley House opposite his yard is a slave to him. If he says he will be leaving for the races at eleven, then time itself seems to wait for him to drive out through the stable gates before the clock chimes the hour.

Neville has always believed in getting up really early in the morning, having a siesta or 'trainer's kip' in the afternoon and then going to bed early at night. The siesta is a cavalry custom because, particularly in hot climates, one would always work through the morning, have lunch and then retire to bed before evening stables. This has become an established practice at Warwick Lodge, and God forbid the man who telephones Neville in the middle of the afternoon!

If anyone in the village keeps him up late at night with rowdy behaviour after the pubs turn out he is not lightly forgiven. The following morning at seven o'clock Neville has been known to go round the houses with his hunting horn blowing a 'Gone away!' and shouting, 'Come on, you idle buggers! Up you get! You kept me awake last night. You can bloody well get up now. Up you get, you idle buggers!'

Surprisingly, everyone in Middleham loves the Captain. Sarah says, 'Dad could never understand why nobody would get up on Christmas morning. After all, that was the day when a jumping trainer had to give his horses a pipe-opener for the big races on Boxing Day. But it seemed that everyone was only interested in opening presents and stockings and he would be off on his horse throughout the village shouting, "Get up, you lazy lot of buggers!"' Then she smiles with pride. 'He's terribly eccentric really, isn't he?'

Like his jockeys, Neville's employees stayed with him indefinitely. The late Bluff Williamson, who died in service as his travelling head man, was a splendid example. Sarah says, 'Bluff was very good to me. I can remember some exceedingly smart owner, perhaps it was the Duke of Roxburghe or someone else pretty high up, coming round with Dad, who heard the clippers going in one of the boxes. He opened the door and said, "And this is where we do the clipping," and there was old Bluff giving one of the apprentices a short back-and-sides!'

Sarah was growing up. She says, 'I never did much riding. It was the one thing that Father really regretted, but he didn't have the time and neither did Mummy. I had an old pony, who was very sweet, and I used to set off with good intentions, but everybody went far too fast for me even up to the moor. Having no brothers or sisters, I wanted to be with everybody doing the same as them, but it was always, "Take the bloody pony away, you're setting everything alight!" I was rather put off. Today Dad admits that it was his fault. I think they were trying to make me run before I could walk.

'My big school was Lawnside in Malvern, only a short way from Cheltenham. That was the only school I really enjoyed. I had a lot of fun there. The day I was confirmed Mother arrived on her own for the confirmation service. When we came out of the church I asked, "Where's Daddy?" Mummy said, "He's at the races. We're going now." I think I must have been the only one who had been confirmed at school, then went off to Cheltenham. It was the Gold Cup meeting. I walked up and there was Dad saddling a horse. He turned round to me and said in broad Yorkshire, "'Ave ya bin dun then?"'

When Neville went down to Lawnside by himself the atmosphere was not easy. 'He was always terrified of the headmistress. She seemed to have the attitude of "You are just a racehorse trainer – pooh!" It was said that she always gave the best sherry to the titled parents, whereas the likes of Father got the cooking sherry out of the kitchen!

'I didn't go abroad for a holiday until I was thirteen. Instead, I used to go to Blackpool with Mum for about a week. Dad would come down for just a weekend. He couldn't stand the fish and chips and all the rest of it. But he would tolerate it. He could just about tolerate one weekend. We stayed in a hotel called the Carlton, I think, and had a super time. We went to shows every single night. I think poor Mum was really worn out at the end of it.'

When Sarah was fifteen, the family went to a fancy-dress ball at Catterick on New Year's Eve. 'Mummy was in a Spanish costume with lots of lace. Dick and Lennie Peacock went with us in the same car. And when we came out at about four o'clock in the morning, you've never seen snow like it! Dad was desperate to get back because of Manchester races the next day. We got stuck between two hills between Middleham and Catterick. We all had to get out and push. Dear old Dick had had a few and, moreover, had light shoes on. Mum's lace thingummy was getting icicles on it. Eventually some army chaps from Catterick came along and got us going. When we got home we changed straight into our racing gear and drove off to Manchester where there was no snow. We had five winners that day!'

In 1957 the two old friends Neville and Fulke Walwyn came into competition again. In the Grand National of 1952 Neville's Teal had defeated Fulke's Legal Joy. Five years later the first big sponsored race in the country was launched by the famous brewers Whitbread, whose boss, Billy Whitbread, was a tremendous National Hunt enthusiast and patron. This time, in their clash over the stiff, exciting Sandown Park course, Fulke was fielding the greatest horse he has ever trained, the brave little bay, Mandarin.

The much heralded Whitbread Gold Cup could hardly have been a greater success. It attracted a vast crowd and resulted in a thrilling finish between Mr H. Draper's Much Obliged, trained by Neville, and Mme K. Hennessy's Mandarin. There were twenty-four starters, and although the fences were stiffer than they are today, only one came to grief.

As Mandarin led Much Obliged by a bare half length at the last fence, those of us who remembered the latter's sensational finishing sprint when making up five lengths from the last to beat Glorious Twelfth by a neck in the Mildmay Memorial on the very same course in the previous January, expected a comfortable win for the Middleham horse. But Mandarin, as ever, was not done by any means and it was neck and neck with fifty yards to go up the steep hill. Once again Much Obliged's sensational turn of foot just prevailed and for a second time he won by a neck.

I always hated seeing Mandarin beaten as he dug up yet

further reserves of courage. But there were many more days for him, in the Cheltenham Gold Cup, the Hennessy Gold Cup and the French Grand National. And this day belonged to Much Obliged and his trainer Neville Crump.

IO

John Penney calls his diary of his time with Neville 'rather a schoolboy's sort of book'. But in fact it shows how a great trainer kept his yard going and how someone like Neville or his contemporary, Noel Murless, has never relaxed. They have had to adapt to modern conditions, but nevertheless they still keep their standards. The lads know where they are. These are the employers whom anyone can understand, particularly when dealing with horses.

I read in John Penney's diary:

1. If a horse is left during trimming, put a rug over it.
2. Clean all feet from the near side.
3. Water as soon as you come in as horses should be cool, having been dismounted and led in.

Here I would add a rider. Atty Persse always insisted that if it was pouring with rain, instead of leading in, you should trot the last ten minutes home so that the horse arrived in the stables warm. Then it was much easier to dry off the most important points, the ears and the loins, leaving the rest to be dried off later. The most important thing, Atty used to stress, was that a horse should arrive home warm. But, on the other hand, nobody was keener than Atty on getting the weight off his horses' backs and on insisting that the lads should lead them home when it was not raining.

4. Horses turned out at grass get one feed of corn in the evening.
5. There should be hay and water in the boxes at all times.
6. A bit is correctly set when it is possible to lay a finger on the bit in the corner of the mouth with ease.

As regards the drill for racing at Warwick House, John Penney has recorded this:

1. Morning feed before race. One bowl of corn and water.
2. Run on an empty stomach.
3. After race hot bran mash. Five of oats to four of bran. Half bucket full – *before* travelling home.
4. Usual meal on arrival home.
5. Finish off day.
6. Disinfectant to be sprayed on straw if horse begins eating it before race. If this is still no good – put on a muzzle.

A few days later he recorded:

1. If a horse goes off his food, it may be for want of a good gallop.
2. Chaff is only used in small quantities on the average. It varies with different horses.
3. You must always clean out the mangers before putting in a new feed.

Of course, as every trainer knows, lads have since the beginning of time had the idea that if a horse leaves anything in his manger it reflects on the lad himself. And, moreover, if they can get to the manger first they will scoop the leavings out onto the floor of the box. But they are only causing harm because if a horse leaves his food, there is usually something wrong with him. Therefore it is vitally important that the head man, or possibly in Neville's case the trainer, should visit each box at least half an hour before the first lad arrives. Then he can see which horses have left their food and make his own deductions, take temperatures, etc.

John writes about sore shins.

If the horse will not let you touch his shins, Fuller's earth and vinegar spread quite thickly over the shins will remedy this.

Fuller's earth and vinegar can also be used for swellings of any kind. Not for lameness.

Toeing. This is when a horse starts kicking his hooves at the trot. The pace is therefore too fast and the horse is not evenly balanced on all fours.

John then writes about grooming, or strapping, horses as he was taught by the Captain.

Like Sir Noel Murless, the Crump hallmarks were patience,

attention to detail and a deep understanding and regard for a horse's nature. Neville started as he meant to go on, as he had learned first of all in the 4th Hussars and then with Sonny Hall at Russley. And he insisted on the old, thorough routine, particularly at evening stables. As modern labour has sadly compelled a relaxation of discipline, litters are no longer picked up at evening stables, horses being inspected instead on their normal beds. It is as well to note here how it was and how indeed it ought to be done.

A fully trained, experienced lad would tie up his first horse and muck out, picking up the clean litter and heaping it up in a smart rectangular pile against the long front wall of the box. He would then spread a thin carpet of straw over the floor and plait the edge by the door, brushing clean the remainder of the sill. Leaving his first horse tied up, he would move on to the second and repeat the process. He would then fetch the necessary hay and new straw for each animal and pile it neatly on the end of the litter. He would have to take his turn with the hoof oil and use it on the hooves of both his horses as and when the oil was free during the evening. This meant that the horses' hooves would have to be picked out ready. Some trainers used a sophisticated mixture containing Stockholm tar, but most thrifty old trainers used sump oil. The hoof is a living thing and the reason for oiling hooves above and below is not so much for smartness as to ensure that the hooves are picked clean and inspected for risen clenches and loose shoes and for any sign of thrush or cracked heels. If necessary the hooves should be treated with medicaments such as Stockholm tar.

Then, going back to the first horse with a bucket half full of water, he would sponge out the eyes, nose and dock in that order. He would now untie the rugs in the reverse order in which he had fastened them, starting with rear straps, then the girth and the breast strap and proceed to groom his horse in quarters, beginning on the near side and always using the hand nearest the horse's head to do the sponging, rubbing or brushing, having rolled the rug back so that it would rest over the animal's loins and quarters. First he would sponge the whole area from the head down the neck to the point where the rug was resting, paying particular attention to sponging out any remaining sweat marks or dung marks which the horse might have collected while he was lying down. Once he had damped the whole area, including the near foreleg, he would dry it briskly with his dry rubber, then, with body brush in the left hand and curry comb in the right, scraping out dirt from the brush at regular intervals, he would brush firmly with a circular motion and then sleek down the coat before throwing the rug forward to cover the part he had just strapped. He would then repeat the performance with the near-side hind quarter and then, putting his horse over, he would repeat the performance on the off side. A good stable man, when strapping a colt or gelding, would probably remove the rug for a few minutes to wisp him thoroughly with a hay wisp to help the circulation. This is not to be done to a filly. After he had finished and put in whatever quarter marks the trainer approved – normally one large sweep was the most effective – he would probably place a clean rubber over the quarters as he replaced the rug, refastening the breast strap and lightly readjusting the girth strap so that it would not mark.

With his dandy brush he would brush out the mane, foretop and tail. Only the head man would use the comb and scissors to bang the tail to the required length. Then he would hurry off to repeat the drill for his second horse. By a quarter of an hour at the latest before the time of the trainer's inspection, he would be finished and both his buckets, now full of clean water, would be lined up with those of the other lads opposite their respective boxes on the other side of the wall. The head man would now ensure that the yard was swept and each lad, himself now clean and tidy, was with his first horse. His grooming kit would be laid out neatly on a stable rubber on top of the litter. The headcollars would have been polished. After the trainer's inspection the lad would bundle up his kit and hurry off to his second horse to await the Guv'nor.

Well, that was how it used to be done. And that was how Neville had been able to keep up the standards throughout his training career, even if lately he has been forced to make compromises. John Penney's diary went on:

Grated carrot and dandelion leaves cut up and mixed with the feed adds to the flavour of the feed. A handful of each. Must be fresh.

1. Don't trot horses downhill as it does them more good to walk. It makes them use their hocks.
2. A corned-up horse will show up his cuts and bruises as the corn generates heat and so makes the injuries swell up. A horse turned out to grass does the opposite.

Then comes a very important point which is all too frequently neglected by even the best jockeys as well as stable lads.

Never stop a horse abruptly after a gallop or a canter. Let him trot on to a walk.

Allowing your horse to trot out must save jarring the fore tendons, but how often do you see jockeys after a race pulling up sharply, perhaps ensuring a breakdown in the future.

When a horse urinates in a box while you are doing him, stand still and let him finish.

Never allow a horse to eat grass while at work as it forms a ball due to the bit and therefore may choke him.

Pull out from the rest of the string before stopping. Never pull up suddenly.

Symptoms of worm – the coat is dull and staring. The horse is not thriving well.

Don't tie a bandage up on the tendon, tie on the side, making no direct strain on the tendon.

If the mane is cut away at the withers, the saddle or rug may start to rub as there is no natural cushion.

Put all dressings on quite flat; avoid creasings, wrinkles, etc.

Never pull a mane or tail when a horse is being fattened up.

When entering stables at stable times, first look into the manger and see if the horse has eaten up, then run your hand down his legs, put on a headcollar and start work.

Count the number of times a horse coughs when out at exercise.

To this I would add, if he coughs more than half a dozen times and fails to blow his nose afterwards, he should go home as he is sickening.

John has also written down a few of the items which worry people who have been born and bred into racing.

A half sister or half brother is when the filly or colt is out of the same dam – no relation if they are by the same sire only. A full sister or brother is by the same dam and sire.

To prevent a horse gobbling up his feed put a few good-sized crushed stones into the manger.

Be sure not to turn out colts with other horses, i.e. mares, fillies and geldings.

Twelve hours' starvation is quite enough before turning a horse out.

A horse should have about twenty minutes' rest between canters.

Some trainers never trot horses.

A cure for sore backs is lead lotion.

Some of these old recipes or prescriptions are far better than the new sophisticated ones.

Schooling over fences at the beginning of the season is quite enough, especially for experienced jumpers.

Never wash a horse's legs that has heel bug as the water feeds the bug.

To this I would add Atty Persse's maxim: 'Never dry legs after you have washed them. Leave them wet.'

Never use new forage. Let all fodder be at least a couple of months old.

Always lunge a horse that has been turned out before you ride him.

It takes a horse ten days to develop a cold, ten days to have it and ten days to get over it.

A blood test is taken from the off side of the neck (tourniquet – syringe – bottle).

After a horse is blistered, he should be kept in for four days and then given light work for a month. If it can be done, he should be turned out a month or so.

When receiving a horse from any source, particularly from another trainer, worm him, physic him ('give him a pink drink') and then start afresh from scratch.

I I

Neville used to pay many shopping visits to Ireland, helped by his great friend, Major Leslie Weaver, one of the best dealers and judges of a jumping horse of our time. But he was equally good at finding horses on this side of the Irish Channel and the first time that he saw Merryman, a huge Scottish bay, Neville was excited by his obvious potential. 'I was at Kelso in 1958 when he won the Buccleuch Hunters Chase by twenty lengths, and from that day I never stopped badgering his owner, Winifred Wallace, to let me train him. Winifred had won three point-to-points on him and in his first season with us he won the Foxhunters at Liverpool and the Scottish National at Bogside by twelve lengths. I always felt he would be my third Grand National winner.'

Merryman's background fulfils all the romantic qualities so often associated with the Grand National. For most of this century Lord Gretton and his family rode to hounds on the descendants of a half-bred mare called The Angel, foaled in the early 1900s. When Lord Gretton died, he passed on two mares to Lord Linlithgow for his daughter, Lady Joan Hope, later to become Lady Joan Gore-Langton. One of them was Maid Marion, the dam of Merryman.

Lord Linlithgow, former Viceroy of India, was not interested in horse breeding and told his daughter to mate Maid Marion as she thought fit. So the mare was sent to the Duke of Northumberland's stallion Carnival Boy (by Colombo), a winner on the flat, over hurdles and over fences, who had been runner-up in the Champion Hurdle of 1946. Merryman was the result of the match. The product of this gift service to a gift mare was foaled and raised on the Hopetoun House estate Near Edinburgh.

A year or two later Lord Linlithgow died and Lady Joan, now married, gave up the family pack of hounds. No clear future was envisaged for Merryman II, as the foal was named. As a green four-year-old he was sent to George Beveridge, landlord of the Plough Hotel at Yetholm and a renowned maker of young horses. Later George was to recall, 'At this point most people thought of him as a prospective hunter. I was asked to find a buyer, but could not do so.'

Miss Winifred Wallace, a long-time subscriber to the Linlithgow pack of hounds, took a fancy to the big bay horse with the white streak down his face. So the new Lord Linlithgow decided not to put Merryman into training and he and his sister sold him for a nominal £470 to Miss Wallace. They kept the price extremely low because Miss Wallace had just lost a couple of good horses and they hoped that Merryman would bring her a change of luck! He certainly did!

Merryman II's path to fame began with Miss Wallace riding him to hounds and then to success in three point-to-points. After he had won a hunter chase at Kelso by twenty lengths in April 1958, his potential was more widely recognized. Miss Wallace therefore sent him to the most respected trainer of jumpers in the country, Captain Neville Crump, early in 1959.

Racing is full of superstitions dating back hundreds of years. For example, a loose one on the gallops in the morning means a winner for the stable that afternoon. Green is an unlucky colour. The late Ossie Bell once seized the green comb produced by the wife of his assistant trainer in the car on the way to the races and hurled it out of the window, even though his most successful colours were the Cunliffe-Owen green and white! You should always try to pass under a train when you are going under a bridge. Innumerable trainers have nearly killed themselves trying to get under a train, particularly under the last carriage or the guard's van! It is very lucky to pass a funeral on the way to the races. And you should never wish an owner, trainer or jockey good luck before a race.

Gerry Scott says, 'I'll never forget Miss Winifred. She was an absolute darling and she would always say the same thing, that she loved her horse and that as long as you came back in one piece it did not matter whether you were first, last or whatever. One day she walked into the paddock and said, "Well, do have a wonderful ride. Good luck." And I said, "Oh, please, don't say that. Don't say that!" Anyway, sure enough we got to the first ditch and, zap, down we came. After that she always came into the paddock and said, "I won't say it! I won't say it!"'

In the seven Grand Nationals between Teal and Merryman the sword of Damocles had been hanging over Aintree and the Grand National. The year after Neville's triumph with Teal, Vincent O'Brien started his famous hat-trick with Early Mist, Royal Tan and Quare Times. In 1954, Royal Tan's year, four horses had been killed, including Teal's runner-up, Legal Joy. Coming so soon after the first-fence calamities and the fiasco of 1951, opposition to the Grand National had been revived. Most of the criticisms were ill-directed, however sincere. The wilder accusations of barbarity were echoes of criticisms made more than a hundred years before. Yet the opposition was powerful enough to get its views expressed in the House of Lords.

Then, in 1956, we saw the almost incredible drama of the Queen Mother's Devon Loch collapsing 50 yards from the post, with the race already won, and a heartbroken Dick Francis walking back to the paddock with the 'winner' who had somehow missed the victory. So Dave Dick on E.S.B. was able to provide Fred and Mercy Rimell with the first of their four Grand National wins.

Nineteen fifty-seven was the year of Fred Winter, the greatest jockey ever seen riding under National Hunt Rules, literally lifting Sundew to victory. Neville's Goosander ran well and got round close up, as he did the following year when the race was won by Mr What. Ken Oliver's Border-trained Wyndburgh, runner-up to Sundew the previous year, now finished fourth and should have won the following year, 1959. Only accident prevented this grand horse and his gallant trainer, now the leading light behind Doncaster Sales, from triumphing. As he jumped Becher's for the second time a stirrup iron snapped. Tim Brookshaw, in his championship season, recovered quickly and slipped the other foot free, riding without stirrups – and, according to Michael Scudamore on Oxo, shouted, 'Look – no feet!' – it should have been the end of Wyndburgh's chances, but Brookshaw never gave in easily. He rode a memorable race, keeping Wyndburgh in touch until Valentine's, then forcing the nine-year-old in pursuit of Oxo between the last two fences. Oxo hit the last, yet stood up. He came away with a long lead, but Wyndburgh whittled it down stride by stride, getting to within two lengths and clinging, never able to quicken yet never yielding. It was a triumph of horse and rider over adversity and both must be numbered amongst the Aintree immortals.

That only four of thirty-four got round sparked off a new controversy. Changes were demanded in the weights and in the construction of the fences. The controversy, rising at times to hysteria, brought to an end a troubled decade at Aintree. Another was about to begin which would make the National a European as well as a nationwide event, and which would see Russian horses competing for the first time. During the next few years the future of Aintree racecourse would be discussed in newspapers, weighing rooms, pubs, clubs and finally the House of Lords.

The Grand National of 1960 was the last to be run over the old, formidable upright fences. It is significant that all Neville's three Grand National triumphs have been achieved over the great obstacles. And this time a new element had arrived – television.

Successive governments had always recognized the fact that 'all work and no play makes Jack a dull boy' and that the most popular spectator sports were football and racing in that order. Long before Bud Flanagan and the Crazy Gang, the winner of the 2.30 had been part of music-hall lore. In the mid-sixties, when the circulation of the *Daily Mail* was $1\frac{3}{4}$ million, we held a reader survey which showed that out of that number 600,000, or just over a third, read about racing. Those who did read it very thoroughly. The others did not read it at all. But in the case of the Derby and the Grand National the whole country has always liked to have a bet.

Furthermore, it is well known that, for excitement, jumping

far outstrips the flat. This knowledge is not only confined to those who have been lucky enough to participate in both sports physically. There is absolutely no doubt that the thrills and spills of steeplechasing – even, to be a bit macabre, the injuries and the possibility of death – excite the public imagination. Unhappily this knowledge was mainly confined to people who live in the country. Most townsfolk had no idea of the sheer, unmitigated joy of a day's cross-country racing on a lovely course like Wincanton, Ludlow, Towcester or Kelso. They knew nothing of the excitement that made National Hunt racing not only the finest sport but also the one sport in the whole world in which Britain excels above all others. Now, for the first time, the Grand National was to be televised and the world's greatest steeplechase was to be brought in all its glory to the firesides of the world.

National Hunt racing had first been televised in January 1948, when the BBC took cameras to Sandown Park. They relayed two steeplechases and a hurdle race, and the response was immediate. Viewers discovered that steeplechasing is a much more exciting and rewarding spectacle than the flat, full of danger and courage, compelling involvement without the need to bet and so fraught with surprises that no horse is believed to be a certainty.

The BBC understood the possibilities, but the development of its service was slow. It was not until the late 1950s that television was available in all parts of Britain and by then commercial television had established itself. On both channels National Hunt racing was a top attraction.

Televising the Grand National presented special problems, but in 1960 the BBC overcame them for the first time. The race was undoubtedly a natural, commanding an estimated audience of 10 million, excluding the millions in other countries who watched through the Eurovision link. If the ghost of William Lynn, who had founded the race as well as the Waterloo Cup all those years ago, had been alive, he would have been fascinated and delighted, for what he had visualized as a national event, appealing to people from all walks of life, had become international in a way beyond his wildest dreams.

The first commentators were Peter O'Sullevan, Clive Graham and Peter Bromley, an accomplished team, bringing to racing a professionalism which the BBC had not at that time always showed in other sports. Peter Montague-Evans and Derek Hart also took part and the producers were Ray Lakeland, Dennis Monger and John Vernon. Suddenly, at the turn of a switch, the race was there, with its exciting build-up beforehand, in every living room in the country. Jockeys and horses who had been only names on the sports pages became alive. The huge legendary fences became real at last. The largest audience for any steeplechase in the world watched the preliminaries for the 1960 race, aware that they were seeing much more of this wonderful spectacle than those who were on the course.

On the night before the race, when the rest of us, having filed our copy, were enjoying ourselves at the Adelphi, Peter, who wrote for the *Daily Express*, went out and dined alone, spending the whole of that evening mugging up the colours for his superb commentary on the Grand National.

For Gerry Scott and Neville Crump it had been an anxious week. Gerry says, 'I broke my collar bone in two places on the Monday at Doncaster and then again on the Saturday, just one week before the race. I was lucky because I went to a physiotherapist for heat treatment. On the Tuesday I was supposed to ride out for the Captain and, thank God, he was away. I told Jack Douglas, the head man, "It's useless. No good," and I went back to the physiotherapist for more heat treatment twice a day. He went mad when I told him I hoped to ride in the National, but he had to strap me up.

'On Thursday I telephoned the Captain and he said, "Look, I have two in hurdle races at Liverpool on Friday. Come up and ride them and see what it's like." I rode the first one and I wasn't too happy at all. But it wasn't so bad with the second. So the Captain said, "Being very, very fair to you, the owner and the public, we will have you before three doctors tonight." The first one came to me and said, "Does this hurt?" and there I was trying to smile. He passed me and so did the second one. But the third one asked, "When did this happen?" I said, "Last

Monday," and he immediately said, "I'm an orthopaedic surgeon. It's quite impossible. You cannot ride. No way." But the Guv'nor said, "The other two doctors passed you and so it's two to one against. So you will ride." So I did.

'Johnny East obviously felt very let down in one respect and it was most embarrassing for me because I'd robbed him of a ride on the National favourite. But Merryman had always been my ride.'

The Grand National field of twenty-six was the smallest since Troytown had won forty years earlier, and the book-makers, particularly in the North, knew that they were onto a hiding after another heavily backed, Middleham-trained horse, Sam Hall's Mustavon, won the Lincolnshire Handicap. The inevitable 'M' syndrome went Middleham – Mustavon – Merryman. So Neville Crump's big horse started favourite at odds of only 13–2. In the parade Merryman, dwarfing his rivals, looked superb, and no one could have told that, under the Wallace tartan sash of his colours, Gerry's collarbone was heavily strapped.

Neville had achieved a near miracle in getting Merryman to the post fit to run for his life. It had been a much closer call than any of us knew. After an inexplicable failure in the Rhymney Breweries Chase at Chepstow in December, Merryman was sent to the Veterinary College at Edinburgh where an inflamed bone in one of his forefeet was diagnosed. His shoes were removed and a long rest completed the cure. Nevertheless there had been time only for one preparatory race before the National, and to produce him looking so superb and fit to win was a triumphant piece of training.

It was a typically cool, grey Liverpool afternoon. The going was fast, visibility reasonably good and the crowd, not surprisingly, had been thinned by the lure of television. The Home Secretary, Rab Butler, was there to decide for himself about the opposition to the Grand National, which had, once again, reached a climax. The oldest rider in the contest, a grey-haired Irishman in his fifties, Mr Burke, attracted attention as he stood coolly smoking a pipe outside the weighing room. Before the race Lord Sefton and the National Hunt

Stewards addressed the assembled jockeys, warning them against the fast going and against the traditional helter-skelter charge to the first fence.

Gerry said later, 'After Lord Sefton had spoken to us all before the race about not crowding on the inside I was prepared to go a bit wide first time round. But all the others seemed to be doing that, so I went on the inner and stayed there all the time. I had no trouble from the other horses.'

So they lined up and set off at a far more reasonable pace than usual. Lotoray, a very forlorn hope, was the only horse down at the first fence and there had been surprisingly little trouble as the field approached Becher's with Green Drill leading from Tea Fiend, Sabaria and Arles, with Merryman and Mr What nicely placed.

The previous year there had been a holocaust at Becher's. This time the only casualties were Wyndburgh and Knox Town. Wyndburgh had jumped over 120 Aintree fences previously without coming to grief. Now, partly unsighted, he jumped too short to reach the level ground. Game as ever, the good horse threw out a despairing leg to save himself, but it was too late. His wiry body screwed in the effort of recovery and although he did not come right down no one could have stayed in the saddle. Wyndburgh went gaily on round and cleared Becher's the second time without touching a twig. He must remain in the history books as one of the finest Aintree performers and the best horses never to win a National.

Not that he would have beaten mighty Merryman on this occasion. Merryman got a bit close to Becher's and pitched on landing, but his great shoulders saved him. Out shot a leg and he was on his way again with barely a pause. It was at the next fence, seemingly innocuous by the standards of Becher's and the Chair, that Merryman made his one bad mistake. Gerry said, 'He fiddled Becher's each time, but it was at the fence after it that he was nearly on his nose. I thought he was sure to go, but he recovered cleverly. I have a photograph which shows his head right behind his forelegs. Remarkable.'

Dandy Scot came down at the Canal Turn and at this point

Tea Fiend was in front. Passing the stands he led from Merryman, Badanloch, Green Drill, Cannobie Lee, Clear Profit, Mr What and Eagle Lodge. In fact twenty horses were still standing as they galloped onto the racecourse, a far higher proportion than usual, but now the pace, sensible as it had been, was beginning to tell. Holly Bank and Uncle Whiskers disappeared at the Chair, where Bellsize II, refusing at the fence, stumbled into the ditch, broke his leg and had to be destroyed. This accident, tragic as it was, could hardly be blamed on Aintree. The Chair looks terrifying from the ground but horses usually jump it well and Bellsize had done so the previous year. After only 2 miles at a steady pace he should not have been exhausted; the slip which cost him his life could have happened on any racecourse in the world.

Coming to Becher's again Tea Fiend still led from Merryman and Badanloch, with Mr What in fourth place. The first three sailed over but Mr What met the fence all wrong: he got over, but fell on landing. Team Spirit, destined four years later to be Fulke Walwyn's only National winner, came down with Pendle Lady, and Cannobie Lee refused, pitching David Nicholson over his head in a spectacular, if ignominious, fashion!

From Valentine's Merryman and Badanloch drew clear of the remainder. Merryman was always going the better and, jumping the last with supreme authority, increased his lead on the run-in to win by fifteen lengths amid a storm of well-earned cheers. Badanloch was twelve lengths ahead of Clear Profit, who passed the gallant front-running Tea Fiend at the last fence.

So ended a wonderful triumph for owner, trainer and jockey in the finest traditions of the sport. It had not been perhaps the most spectacular National ever, but one in which almost every horse had had a chance if he had been good enough.

As for the ungenerous, inaccurate and unworthy accusations that it was run at a 'crawl' to impress the television audience or the Home Secretary, Merryman's time – 9 minutes 27 seconds, which is well up to the average of the race – gives the lie to that. Moreover the winner was travelling so easily for the last mile and won with so much in hand that, if he had been pushed, the time would have been even faster.

It was estimated that between 13 and 15 million viewers had seen the race. That was the unofficial estimate of the audience for the BBC's history-making broadcast of the Grand National. Final viewer research figures for the venture proved that the broadcast was a big success with the continental countries that saw it. Within a few minutes of the end of the broadcast the BBC received congratulatory calls from abroad.

The Home Secretary had gained his first impressions of the race at Aintree. A carefully worded statement from a press officer speaking for Mr Butler afterwards said: 'As far as he could see (and this was only half an hour after the race) there was nothing objectionable in the race.' In ten minutes Merryman had done more for the cause of the world's greatest steeplechase than anyone since it started in 1839.

I can do no better than to quote the typically excellent summary written by John Oaksey as Audax in *Horse and Hound*.

The Grand National was in the dock on Saturday – like a man fighting for his life on a capital charge, with a tide of circumstantial evidence rising against him. And, as the twenty-six horses faced the tapes at Aintree, the prosecution may well have felt themselves nearer to securing a conviction for cruelty than ever before in their long well-meant crusade. Ten minutes later a big bay horse with a white face had galloped home in triumph and the case had swung dramatically in favour of the accused. One horse, it is true, lay dead, but the race, as a whole, had been free of the fickle wholesale disasters on which its opponents based their claims.

Of the fourteen horses who fell (eight finished and three were pulled up and one refused), not more than two were brought down through no fault of their own. No jockey was seriously injured and millions of people watching on television had seen a unique and thrilling sight – a sight by which the most devoted animal lover could hardly be offended.

I do not mean to imply that the organisations opposing the Grand National are wanting the worst to happen, nor do I suppose that their opposition will cease forthwith. But I do sincerely believe that we saw clear proof on Saturday that this is not an unfair test for suitable horses. With a field of this size (thirty, I feel, should be the limit in future) and with jockeys who use their common sense, the Grand National is neither unnecessary nor dangerous.

The vast publicity given by the BBC's skilful, well-planned broadcast can only have strengthened its hold on the public's imagination and its future is now more safely assured than seemed likely or even possible before the race.

When interviewed after the race Gerry Scott said emphatically, 'There's nothing wrong with the course at all. But I think they might make the qualifying conditions a bit stricter.'

He says now, 'Merryman jumped absolutely brilliantly. Going to the Canal second time round, we had two horses in front of us and it is amusing how little things flash through your mind. We were going to go between them, which could have proved fatal, but then at the last moment we switched to the inner. It's funny how at such speed things flash through your mind.'

Racing has always been a great leveller. After all the congratulations and celebrations, Gerry went to Worcester on the following Monday where Neville had four runners all ridden by him, all favourites. 'I had to pull the first one up and the next two fell. So then I didn't ride the fourth. Fancy that happening just two days after winning the National!'

Poor Gerry. One of the finest jockeys ever to ride a steeplechaser was to have his career ruined by injury from now on. He says, 'I saw that season out, and when Merryman had his first race after the National at Wetherby on Boxing Day of the same year, 1960, I won on him with top weight of 12 st 6 lb. I completed a double on another of the Captain's horses, Mack's Leap, in the novice chase, and the following day, after finishing second on Tin-Tacks, I won the big chase on Fort Dawn. But then, in the last, the novice hurdle, challenging desperately at the last, we came down and I broke my leg. Trying to get back in action in time to partner Merryman again in the Grand National, I rode an aptly named horse called Careless Lord in the novice hurdle, the first race on the card at

Newcastle on 11 March. We were going really well with the leader when he made a bad mistake three hurdles out from which he didn't recover and he fell at the last, breaking my leg again.'

Gerry broke a leg six times – one four times and the other twice. So for the next two years he was virtually out of action.

12

It was in November 1960, five weeks before Gerry's last ride on his Grand National winner, that Neville sent Merryman for a preliminary race to Uttoxeter. The great chaser with his wonderful low action loathed soft going. One of the most stupid sayings in racing – and God knows there are plenty of them – always delivered with great authority, is 'A good horse acts on any going'. This is complete rubbish. An animal with a sweeping, daisy-cutting action can obviously not gallop in a ploughed field. On the other hand, a horse with a high knee action is equally ill at ease on hard going. He cannot bang his legs down on ground like brick.

On the morning of the meeting there was such a deluge that the late Gay Sheppard, Clerk of the Course, told me that in all his experience he had seldom seen worse going. 'But, believe it or not, there was no rain up to nine o'clock this morning,' said Gay, 'and conditions were good. Since then it never stopped. By 11.30, when it was obvious it was going to be very heavy, it was too late to call the meeting off.'

Unfortunately owner, trainer and horse had to travel a long distance to Uttoxeter. Miss Winifred Wallace drove 300 miles from over the Border and Neville, with his wife Brownie, motored 160 miles from Middleham. As Neville arrived at the course he was greeted by Bluff Williamson, who told him that he had declared Merryman as a runner. (In those days there were still no overnight declarations.) This was too much. Neville's language in such circumstances has never been mild. He burst out, 'What the —— hell did you do a thing like that for? We'll ruin him for good if we run him in this.'

A policeman directing the traffic looked in at the window of the car. ''Ere, 'ere, 'ere!' he said sternly. 'You can't go using language like that.'

To which Neville replied promptly, 'Well, it's a pretty poor state of affairs if a chap can't say what he wants to his own wife!'

In the event, after a consultation with the owner and with jockeys who had ridden in the first race, Neville and Gerry decided not to run.

After his Wetherby success Neville gave Merryman one more run before the National, at Doncaster on 4 February, in the Great Yorkshire Chase, which has never been a lucky race for the Captain. Ridden by Johnny East, carrying 11 st 6 lb and starting favourite at 2–1, the big horse was left with far too much to do after lying out of his ground, and although he made up a great deal of the leeway he could finish no better than fifth. It may have appeared a trifle disappointing but, as he was only six lengths behind the great Mandarin, who was giving him just 4 lb, it cannot have been too bad an effort.

The run-up to the 1961 Grand National was certainly the most interesting that I have ever known, probably because the prizemoney had jumped from £13,134 in 1960 to £20,020 – an astonishing figure in a sport which still had steeplechases worth less than £200 to the winner. Part was contributed by the organizers, part by the Irish Hospitals Sweepstake, which had been contributing since 1958, and for the first time a commercial company added £5000. That company was Messrs Schweppes, a generous sponsor of National Hunt races.

The fences had been altered, partly in deference to criticism, but chiefly in the hope of attracting top-class steeplechasers to Aintree. Neville's friend and owner, Wing Commander Peter Vaux, the senior capped National Hunt Steward, supervised a change of shape. Hitherto the fences had been upright. Now they were sloped on the take-off side, well bushed out, giving a horse another yard in which to see the fence and time his take-off. Many falls had been caused less by inability to jump than by horses getting too deep. The top weight had been lowered to 12 stone. These measures, while welcomed all round, had one urgent purpose, to persuade owners and trainers that good horses could be fairly risked at Aintree.

These moves met with great success. The top French amateur, thirty-six-year-old René Couetil, with 250 winners under both Rules to his credit, brought over his big bay, Imposant, to qualify with the necessary three runs before the handicap was published. Otherwise, without running in England or Ireland, his horse would have had to carry top weight.

Above all, this was the year of the Russian invasion. They sent over the three best chasers – Grifel, Reljef and Epigraff – behind the Iron Curtain to challenge for the Grand National. Sadly, what was considered by some to be a courageous sporting venture was, in fact, a disappointing enterprise, doomed from the start to end in humiliation. At the end of their five-day journey across Europe, my fellow journalists and I were introduced to the three horses and their riders. Clearly, despite their successes behind the Iron Curtain, they were all about the standard of middling point-to-point performers. Yet here they were, in the home of steeplechasing, preparing to compete against the best human and equine professionals in the world's greatest steeplechase.

'Time spent in reconnaissance is seldom wasted' is one of the oldest cavalry precepts. Uncharacteristically, from what we had always believed of them, the Russians had done none. They should have known that, without a run over here, their horses would automatically have to carry the top weight of 12 stone, and that, over 4½ miles, 2 lb is the equivalent of about two lengths. A short while before the race I went up to Haydock to report on them for the *Daily Mail* and was amazed by what I saw. The riders did not dress like jockeys, but as if they were going for a hack on Hampstead Heath. Only two horses went to the post because Epigraff was lame. Reljef and Grifel, ridden by Boris Ponomarenko and the champion of all Russia, Vladimir Prakhov, respectively were compelled to give weight to three previous winners of the National, 2 lb to Neville Crump's mighty Merryman, 5 lb to Mr What and 6 lb to Oxo. Both were entire horses, a grave disadvantage over these big fences because stallions inevitably scratch their 'undercarriages'. In my lifetime the only stallion to succeed in the National was the gallant little American Battleship, ridden by Bruce Hobbs in 1938. Grifel, a golden chestnut, stood just about 16 hands; Reljef, a medium bay, was only 15.3 hands. In their company Merryman, standing over 17 hands and full of power, would have looked like Rocky Marciano at a debs' dance.

Half an hour after the last race on the first day of the Liverpool meeting Vladimir Prakhov and Boris Ponomarenko stood in the weighing room earnestly asking Laurie Morgan how to ride the National course. They had just seen the Australian Olympic champion win the Foxhunters Chase for the second time. He explained to the Russians that the Chair was, in his opinion, the worst obstacle on the course. They told him through their interpreter that Becher's Brook, where they had seen three horses fall, was the fence that was giving them a headache. They said that it was the only fence they feared and, because of their concern over it, certain arrangements had been made for them to have 'grandstand' seats beside it for the two big races on the third day over the National fences.

That night, back at their hotel on Haydock racecourse 20 miles from Aintree, the Russians held an inquest on what had caused the three horses to fall. The jockeys paced their long, narrow dining room, reasoning out the crashes. By now they must have realized that their horses and they themselves would be hopelessly outclassed and overfaced in attempting to jump Aintree fences at racing speed.

For the great race itself the Russian riders discarded their suburban hacking attire and adopted even more way-out costume. John Hislop wrote in the *Observer*:

> When the horses came into the paddock, the centre of interest was the Russian pair Reljef and Grifel. Neither looked the part for the job, being typical flat-race horses, and Reljef, a light-framed little bay, looked barely big enough and strong enough to jump puddles.
>
> Both entires, they carried a bloom on their coats which geldings do not have, but neither was well groomed or well turned out.

With their manes unplaited and their tails long and untrimmed, sporting rawhide bridles and circular steel metal discs on the headpiece just below the ears, they had an oriental air about them.

Reljef is a neat little horse with an attractive head and slightly lopears. His stable companion, Grifel, is bigger and stronger, but rather plain about the head, with a wall eye, a crooked near foreleg and a slight stringhalt.

The Russian riders also attracted interest and attention. More heavily built than their English counterparts, especially Prakhov, Grifel's jockey, they presented a rather strange sartorial picture, as they did not wear the usual white neck-scarf used by English riders, nor the elastic bands round the wrists to keep the sleeves of the jacket from flapping about; as a result they looked as if they were wearing pyjama jackets. Ponomarenko, Reljef's jockey, wore a stylish pair of boots, their tops being of white leather with the lower edge generously waved, giving them the appearance of being part of a circus rider's attire.

It was obvious to Neville and the other English professionals that they had nothing to fear from the Russian challenge.

Neville, hoping against hope that Gerry would be able to partner Merryman again, had allowed Johnny East to take the ride on Bobby Renton's Ernest, who had won the Grand Sefton Chase over the Aintree course in Mrs Brotherton's colours. So, after Gerry's Newcastle fall, Neville engaged Derek Ansil, an excellent horseman and, in the circumstances, as good a substitute as could be found for Gerry Scott.

In Gerry's enforced absence Neville had, in fact, approached Ryan Price for the services of Fred Winter, but Ryan had bought Kilmore shortly before the race and, to Fred's dismay at the time, he had to ride the little bay horse. He admitted afterwards that he was highly surprised by Kilmore's performance and said that, had he known him better and had more confidence in his ability, he would have finished considerably closer than fifth.

It was a lovely clear day as the thirty-five runners paraded in front of the stands. Paradoxically it was not a mishap at a fence but a dramatic incident at the line-up for the start which, in retrospect, probably affected the final result, a result which prevented Neville from equalling Aubrey Hastings's record of four Grand Nationals and ironically helped his friend, that wonderful trainer, the late Fred Rimell, towards that elusive target.

The jockey who tells you that he is not nervous before the Grand National is notable rather for his mendacity than for his courage. At the start every heart beats faster, every mouth is dry and every laugh is a little forced as you gaze down the Aintree back stretch and think of the 4½ gruelling miles ahead. There are the loose horses, fallers, injuries. There may even be dead horses and maimed jockeys. You have to be good to get round, but, even more, you have to be lucky. As they circle around and begin to line up, nerves are on edge and the feeling is carried down the reins to the horses. It was here that millions of television spectators and the crowds on the grandstands saw Merryman wince at the unexpected impact of a vicious double-barrelled broadside delivered by the heels of the 40–1 amateur-ridden outsider Jimuru. Derek Ancil promptly waved an appeal to the starter, Alec Marsh, for some moments' delay while the damage was appraised. Mr What's rider, Dave Dick, a close-up eyewitness, said, 'It sounded like a pistol crack and the effect was as if Merryman had been branded.'

After inspection, however, it was decided all was well. Merryman was put back into the line-up and showed no ill effects. In the circumstances he ran a tremendously brave race, which was a credit to his own courage and to the ability of his trainer and jockey. The ground was right, very fast, and before the jockeys left the weighing room they had, as in the previous year, been warned by Lord Sefton against a mad-dash Charge of the Light Brigade on the long run to the first fence.

When the tapes went up they set off at a good but sensible gallop. When the final shape of the race began to form, as it nearly always does after Becher's has been jumped for the second time, Merryman's supporters had great hopes. He was going really well in the lead, jumping boldly, accurately and fast with no sign of weakening. When Fresh Winds fell, he was left in front of Nicolaus Silver, Wyndburgh, O'Malley Point,

Scottish Flight and Kilmore. This bunch were well clear of the remainder.

As they rounded the Canal Turn the second time and headed for home, the race looked to be between Merryman, Kilmore, Nicolaus Silver and Scottish Flight, who was going well for Bill Rees. But in that reasonably good visibility for Aintree we could see that the young Irish champion jockey, Bobby Beasley, on Fred Rimell's grey, Nicolaus Silver, was going really well within himself.

Three fences out Scottish Flight made a bad mistake, but he would not have won in any case. As the runners headed for the race course after jumping the last fence in the country, it still looked to be anybody's race. Although Merryman was going as strongly as ever, Nicolaus Silver was moving up ominously; Kilmore was still a fighting force, while O'Malley Point was creeping up on the heels of the leaders and Wyndburgh was plugging safely along, ready to take advantages of any falls in front of him.

At the second last Merryman was still in front and on the stands his supporters were beginning to cheer the prospect of the first double victory since Reynoldstown. He landed two lengths clear of Nicolaus Silver, with Kilmore almost upsides and O'Malley Point trying to join them.

The grey took the lead at the last with Merryman trying desperately to get back on terms. But Bobby Beasley kept Nicolaus Silver going so well and, by some strange instinct inherited perhaps from his grandfather, Harry, who had won the 1891 National on Come Away, he seemed to know that on this occasion the middle of the course was the better way and, leaving the rails to Derek Ansil, rode Nicolaus Silver home to a five-length victory. O'Malley Point just got the better of Scottish Flight by a neck for third place and brave little Kilmore, eleven years old, was fifth. The time of the race, 9 minutes 22⅗ seconds, was only 2⅕ seconds slower than Golden Miller's record in 1934. Fourteen finished – the largest number to do so the previous decade.

The Russians? Well, although Vladimir Prakhov and Grifel came to grief at Becher's first time, the Russian rider was determined to have his round and Grifel was sent after the field a long way behind. The others were almost out of sight when Grifel reappeared in front of the stands, made a fair old mess of the Chair, ran out by mistake on to the other course, was brought back to make a second jump at the water and was then pulled up.

His companion, Reljef, set off in the rear of the field and was soon tailed off. The jockey was unseated at Valentine's first time round. Ponomarenko said later that a loose horse cut across him and that that was the cause of the trouble.

When Merryman, the heroic runner-up, returned to the enclosure with a grapefruit-sized bruise from Jimuru's vicious kick on his quarter, both Miss Winifred Wallace and Neville sportingly discounted suggestions that the blow had been responsible for their champion's defeat. But no one had noticed or suspected at the time that Jimuru had landed with both left and right heels – the left connecting with the point of Merryman's stifle bone. The undetected injury was certainly more serious and much more painful than the lump raised on the quarter.

The next day Neville reported, 'Merryman was stiff and sore when led up this morning. I still don't want to make an issue of it, but there is no doubt it could have made a lot of difference.' Neville added that this blow to the leg could have caused Merryman to hang sideways on the run-in and to finish so much more distressed than the previous year.

Merryman had given his all. The race had strained his great heart almost to the limit. Neville says, 'Merryman was never any good afterwards.' He died in November 1966 at a meet of the North Northumberland hounds.

Today, good as Teal was, there is no doubt in the Captain's mind that Merryman II was the best of his National winners. 'Teal might have been more brilliant, but Merryman was the ideal horse for Liverpool,' he says. 'Half lame, he finished second to Nicolaus Silver carrying a stone more than when he won it and ridden by an unfamiliar jockey.' He adds, 'There always seems to be one decent horse let in down the handicap, as Nicolaus Silver was with 10 st 1 lb.'

There have been no more Aintree Grand National winners for Neville – yet. Forest Prince finished third to Fred Winter's Anglo with Gerry Scott up in 1966, the year when Much Obliged, his stable companion, fell at the third fence. Goosander was probably unlucky not to win.

Gerry Scott recalls the occasion when Neville was stopped going into the carpark at Liverpool and the gateman asked his name. Neville, amazed that, after all these years, anyone, particularly at Aintree, should not recognize him, said, 'Who the hell do you think I am? I'm Neville Crump. I've trained three Grand National winners here.'

The boy said, 'Oh yeah? That's what the last guy said to me who came in here with his car.'

Unbeknown to Neville, he had followed Fred Rimell into the carpark.

13

Looking back, Neville comments on the Grand National at Liverpool. 'They have won in all shapes and sizes,' he says. 'They don't have to be as big as a house – Battleship was only 15 hands, Teal was only a shade over 16.1. But Merryman was 17 hands or more. Battleship was an entire horse, which made his a remarkable performance. But you can't lay down any hard and fast rules about the making of a National horse. There certainly isn't a typical Aintree type – but there may be typical Aintree horses.

'What a horse needs more than anything is a good, bold outlook and plenty of guts. And if he's going to win, the jockey needs guts as well. And it's an extraordinary thing about the National that, although the race is the longest under Jockey Club Rules, it seems a horse doesn't have to be an out-and-out stayer to win the race. Take George Owen's Russian Hero – they thought he wouldn't get more than two miles, but of course he won.'

This has always been Fred Rimell's theory. He said, 'Two and a half miles is not racing distance and neither is four and a half miles. This is why horses like Russian Hero and my Gay Trip, top-class two and a half mile horses, can win the National.' Of course, the obvious alternative is the out-and-out stayer.

Neville says, 'I've had horses which have been favourites or near favourites to win the National. Goosander was one. We thought he would stay for ever, but when he got to the point where they come on the racecourse with about half a mile to go, he had nothing left. It's the last half mile that finds many of them out. The race is peculiar in that on the day a horse either falls down terrified to death or produces form which he never produced before. And I don't think that it's the course which has this effect. It's the crowd and the parade and atmosphere and all that sort of thing. It makes a horse either show his ability, or it can make him funk and go the other way.

'And I'm not sure that I agree that previous visits to the course mean all that much. Quite a number of horses have won on their first visit to Aintree. Others have plugged away year after year without winning. When I trained Wot No Sun, he ran a number of times in the National, finishing second and third to Freebooter and Teal respectively. That's pretty good Aintree form, but he never came first.

'As regards the smaller Aintree races, Roughan won the Topham Trophy – twice I think – but I never ran him in the National because I didn't think he'd get more than two miles. Had I done so it might have been another Russian Hero. I think the Foxhunters Chase can be a stepping stone to the National for a certain type of horse. I won it with Merryman II, but besides being a hunter and a point-to-pointer, he was a horse and a half. Generally speaking I'm against a horse running in a four-mile race as part of his preparation for the National. The Eider Chase at Newcastle, or whatever it has now been renamed under sponsorship, is invariably won on soft or heavy going, and a horse can lose the National by winning the other race. A horse who wins the National must be fresh. And in the present-day Nationals a horse must have had some experience in handicap company after his novice days.

'The National is full of contradictions – in fact when I said you can't lay down any hard and fast rules about the conformation of National horses, I should have said you can't lay down any hard and fast rules about the National.

'For instance, sometimes horses are chancy jumpers on park courses but won't take the slightest chance when they come to Aintree, and the converse can also be true. Some horses, as you know, never won another race after they won the National. Others only produce their best form at Aintree. And yet others show signs of running in the National for a long time. As I said earlier, Merryman was never any good after finishing second in the race the year after he had won it. But then there were extenuating circumstances. I like a horse that's got recent form but hasn't had too much racing during the earlier half of the season.

'A lot can depend on jockeyship if certain circumstances prevail. I've seen a jockey win the race by kidding another jockey into losing it. But, of course, they can't win without the right horse – and a good slice of luck.'

The year after Merryman's gallant failure, the National was won by Ayala, trained by Keith Piggott and ridden by another fine jump jockey, Pat Buckley. Pat had served his apprenticeship with Neville at Warwick House from 1957 to 1962 and rode his first winner in 1962 in his first ride over fences. Opportunities came early to him owing to the repeated injuries to Gerry Scott, and Pat did not waste them. His other important winners for Neville included Arcturus in the 1968 Scottish Grand National, which Neville has now won five times, the 1963 Whitbread Gold Cup on Hoodwinked, and the Whitbread again in the following year on Dormant, who also won the Mildmay Memorial that season. In the second Whitbread, in which he beat Fulke Walwyn's famous Mill House by three lengths, Pat had had to waste so stringently to get down to 9 st 7 lb that he was barely able to stand while the Queen Mother made the presentation. Injury forced Pat's retirement in 1976.

Daughter Sarah was by now a 'blossoming', as she says, young woman. One of the finest cavalry regiments in the world, the 'Cherry Pickers', the 11th Hussars (Prince Albert's Own), was stationed at Carlisle and some of the young officers spent as much time as they could with Neville at Middleham, riding out whenever possible. Among them were Tim Forster, who has now equalled Neville's score of three Grand National winners, and Sir Phillip Payne-Gallwey, a keen and effective amateur rider and now director of the British Bloodstock Agency. Sarah says, 'They kept wanting to take me out, but didn't quite know how to tackle Dad!'

One day at Carlisle races from the top of a stand Neville saw a posse of young officers chatting up Sarah down below. He bellowed, 'Lay off, you young buggers! My daughter's not going to marry some impoverished cavalry officer. My daughter's going to marry a man with real money. A man with a French-letter factory!'

At that time there was a horse in the yard called Rock's Cross, a bad traveller, who needed a companion. The press got hold of the story and Sarah was pictured in the tabloids with horse and goat. That night after dinner in the mess Bunny McCalmont's brother, Major Dick Sutton, the second in command of the 11th, said, 'Bring me a bit of paper.' He wrote:

> Dear Captain Crump,
> Our horses do not travel well.
> From the *Sketch* and from the *Mirror*
> We see that you have found the spell.
> Will you help us very quick?
> Otherwise we'll miss the boat.
> Send us now your charming daughter.
> You can keep the bloody goat!
> Hoping you will grant this loan,
> Best of luck, Prince Albert's Own.

Sarah says, 'When he received this, Dad gave such a roar of delight he nearly blasted down Middleham!'

When Sarah learned to drive Neville was particularly nervous. 'Mum was away and, of course, you had to have someone sitting with you. Dad used to make me drive him over to Ilkley, but beforehand he would always say, "Go back and get a roll of loo paper to take with us." Every time. It was a bit unnerving having a roll of loo paper in the car. Never known him so nervous!

'Then I had a boyfriend called Jeremy, who was related to Peter Vaux and was as mad as a hatter. When I first asked Dad if he could come and stay – he used to tease me unmercifully about anything of that kind – he said, "Yes, but he's bloody staying in a box outside!"

'We used to call this boy Chipmunk, so Dad painted "Chez Chipmunk" in red paint on the door of the box. Then he got a

163

halter and the box set fair and bedded down all ready. When this poor boy got out of his car you can imagine how terrified he was in any case – he was only about eighteen – and Dad led him straight into the stable to show him where he was going to be bedded down for the night. "Chez Chipmunk" stayed on that door for years. Of course, he was allowed to sleep in the house. It was just Dad's big joke.

'It was awful going out with any young chap because really all they came to do was to see Dad. They used to love it. They used to like listening to his stories and I could never get them out once they got in there. They'd just be sitting there with their mouths open!

'Dad always liked all the parties, of course. At any of the dos it was always jacket off and shirtsleeve order and he was right in there. But now he's slowed down a bit on the parties. I think his last hunt ball was about six years ago. That was the last really big do that he went to. But he's very fond of Bill Cadogan and went to his seventieth birthday party two years ago. But nowadays he doesn't really like being up late. He's usually in bed by nine, but he's awake and his mind is going at six o'clock in the morning. You can't catch him out on the papers or anything like that. He goes through the lot, even today. He always turns to the racing first!'

In the sixties doping, usually by bookmaker-inspired gangs attempting and succeeding in nobbling hot favourites like Noel Murless's Pinturischio, was rife. Sarah recalls, 'One Sunday afternoon when Dad was having his usual kip the doorbell rang and there was a frightfully glamorous woman dripping in mink standing on our doorstep. Mum answered the door and the woman asked whether she could see Neville Crump. Mum thought it was more than her life was worth to wake him up, but, looking at the woman, who was saying that she was very interested in sending not just one but four horses to him, she thought she should.

'Dad was taken completely off his guard. The woman came in and spent most of the afternoon talking. Then they went round the horses and she suddenly became very interested, taking much more interest than normal in which horses were in which boxes. That's looking back, of course – at the time we didn't see anything unusual in it.

'Later, after she'd left, we had a number of telephone calls from other trainers saying that this woman had been to them and had she been to us? So they all reported it and the police finally caught the gang. I went with Dad to Brighton for the case. All the press thought I was his bird!'

Women have always found Neville attractive but he has remained firmly faithful and typically loyal to Brownie throughout their married life. A few years ago, when he was well into his sixties, a very attractive, sexy young lady in her mid-twenties, who, in racing parlance, could be described as 'very hot under the tail', offered herself to Neville. The Captain looked down at her and said, 'No thanks, love. I'll stick to me old lady. You see, I fart in bed and she never complains. So let's leave it at that, shall we?'

Gerry Scott, who told me that story, was determined that it should get into this book because it demonstrates much of the Captain's character.

Neville is particularly proud of daughter Sarah and of her husband Roger, a successful market gardener in the Vale of Evesham near Pershore. He gets tremendous pleasure from his grandchildren. Mandy, who, after working for her grand-father for a while as driver and secretary, is now secretary to Geoff Lewis at Epsom. Sarah says, 'Dad has helped me send Christopher away to school and I can't thank him enough for that. He's so proud that Christopher has inherited his rowing ability. To no mean tune. He won the gold medal in the coxed pairs for the junior national championship and then he won another gold medal as a member of the English team in France. Two golds in two weeks. He is now qualified for Henley. Not bad at the age of eighteen.'

Sarah adds, 'We had one or two good assistant trainers, like Roddy Armytage, who has done so well as a trainer, and Peter Vaux, who was with us for quite a while. Being away at school, I didn't see much of them. But I've always regretted that he has never had anyone younger because, now that he is getting on, obviously it is harder for him. He does insist, as he always has done, on doing it all himself. He never decentralizes. If he had had someone younger with whom he really got on he would have quite enjoyed stepping back. It was only when he was younger that he had the really good assistants.

'Dad has always had a lot of patience with staff. He is very much a one-man band and a perfectionist. He won't let anybody do anything for him really. If my husband, Roger, goes up there and offers to take Dad's old horse out, he always says, "Oh no, I can do that!" He never thinks anyone can do anything as well as he can.'

I thought that now I was getting a little nearer the answer to my question as to why Neville Crump is undoubtedly one of the greatest jumping trainers of all time. Gerry Scott was able to put his finger on it when he said, 'The Captain has always been an absolute perfectionist. Nothing is too good for his horses or for those who work for him.'

The 1962 Hennessy Gold Cup is another instance of how Neville stands by his staff. Gerry was again involved. The stable had two strongly fancied horses for the race, Lord Joicey's Springbok and Rough Tweed, who belonged to Neville's old friend Colonel Simon Lycett-Green. Because Gerry was rather accident prone, Lord Joicey was not keen on his riding Springbok and had been trying to persuade Neville to book an outside jockey for the horse. But, as ever, the Captain was adamant. He insisted that, as Gerry was his first jockey, he should have the choice of mounts and when his choice was Springbok his Lordship was predictably none too pleased. As things turned out, Springbok survived a mistake at the last and, in the finest finish in the history of the race, got up in the last stride to beat Rough Tweed, ridden by David Nicholson, by a head.

To win the Hennessy Gold Cup was a triumph indeed, but Lord Joicey was still not satisfied. Neville says, 'He was a miserable old bugger. He telephoned me the following day and said, "I'm glad I won because, if I hadn't, I'd have taken my horses away from you," whereas Simon Green was delighted and told me to treat Rough Tweed as a winner as far as my percentage was concerned.'

And Sarah remembers the day when Neville took Lord Joicey to buy a horse. Just as they were about to leave the house where they were staying, Neville thought, God, I bet the old boy hasn't packed his bag. He went tearing upstairs, found he was right, packed the case and came down. As they were saying goodbye Joicey produced half a crown, gave it to Neville and said, 'Give this to whoever packed my bag.' Neville kept it, quite rightly!

Neville, who is essentially his own man, has never stood any truck from owners, or anyone else for that matter. He himself tells the story of the day, when Edward Heath was Prime Minister. Neville was invited to the Gimcrack dinner at York. 'Our local MP Tim Kitson, a keen racing man, was Heath's right-hand man and lived very close to us. At the dinner there were lots of speeches and, although everyone had drunk an amazing amount of wine, there hadn't been a chance to have a pee. So I was bursting. In the end I got up and walked out! Afterwards they changed the rules and had a ten minutes' break between speeches so that people could go and relieve themselves.

'Anyway, I was peeing away like mad when I was tapped on the shoulder. I turned round and said, "I don't like being tapped on the back while I'm peeing. Go away!" It was our MP. So I said, "Oh, it's you. Wait a minute." He said, "I want to introduce you to the Prime Minister." So I said, "Just a minute, I want to do my flies up!"

'I turned round and sure enough it was Mr Heath. Watching Crump peeing, you see! So I said, "How do you do, sir?" and all that nonsense. And that idiot Timothy said, "This fellow's won three Grand Nationals." So Heath said, "Did you ride them yourself?" I was very fat at that time and said, "Hardly!" He didn't like that at all!

'So after that we went in to the bar and there was Heath again, standing right next to me. So I said, "Excuse me, sir. I think we've got one thing in common." "Good God!" he said. "And what is that?" I said, "We both went to Balliol," He said, "Who was your tutor?" So I said, "Christ! I can't remember!" "Oh," said the Prime Minister and turned away.

He seemed put out. Don't think he liked me very much!'

Gerry Scott describes the Captain's training methods stressing that the key words were patience, loving care, attention to detail and perfection in all things.

'The horses would come up from grass about 20 July. We would trot up the road for one and a half hours every day for six to eight weeks – steady trotting. The Captain rode out every day, which I really admired. A lot of trainers would come up in their cars and say do this, do that, whereas the Captain would be with you on his horse all the time. Whatever the weather, he was there. He still rides out. He insists on trotting slowly and it's very difficult sometimes to set a slow pace when there are a lot of horses in the string. We were always taught to walk fast and trot slowly. We always had running martingales going to the horses' withers. He would work his horses on two weekdays, Wednesday and Saturday. Not a lot of fast work, only ever seven furlongs at the most and always on the bridle. He would never have any off the bridle. You never ever rode out with a whip. When you rode out, except for schooling, even jockeys like Arthur Thompson never rode out with one.

'One thing I didn't like about his programme was the fact that he would school on any day regardless, whereas I didn't like to school on a race morning. But he would if he felt so inclined. I am certain in my own mind it's only a matter of our not getting together and talking about it. There was always a list up on the tackroom wall of who was riding what for schooling, but I never liked schooling on the day of a race. I thought it was unnecessary as there were so many other free days without tempting Providence by taking chances.

'When the horse was schooled it was, of course, Neville Crump's opinion that mattered. We only had one difference in all the time we worked together. It was over a horse called Forecastle, a grey horse. I was getting him to pick up. This was a novice schooling over fences and the thing I liked about schooling was that I loved horses to make mistakes because you then knew how to handle them. A natural jumper who just goes ping, ping can be dangerous. I like them to make mistakes and I knew this Forecastle had to pick up. He was that kind of horse, and this particular day he was wrong at the ditch. I asked him particularly to flex. The Captain went wild. When we went back in, he said, "I would like to have a word with you, Gerry, in the office." He would never talk in the yard. In the office he said, "Look, I would never dream of telling you how to ride a horse," then he gave me his opinion about how to ride that particular horse. We both had a good chat about it and the horse went off to Wetherby for the Mackeson Champion Novices Chase.'

Gerry's luck finally ran out close to home when the string was returning to Warwick House after a morning's work. He says, 'I was one of the instigators of skullcaps for riding out. We only wore skullcaps for schooling in those days. It's ironic, really. It was going to happen. I am a great believer in what will be will be – a fatalist. Only four times in my life can I remember riding the horses into the yard. Usually we led them in but this day it was pouring with rain and the Captain said, "Stay on and keep the tack dry," so we did. Just at the top of the bank there was a garage and a bread van came up. My horse slipped and I ended up on the road. I can't remember much after that.'

He had cracked his skull so badly that there was no question of his carrying on. The doctors forbade it. He says, 'The Captain, doing everything in his power to get me some money, told me to sue him and then he would claim from his insurance company. We got everything going, filled in the necessary forms and the man came round to see me. As he was getting up to go he said, "Well, that's all right. There should be no hitch about that. You should be able to get a tidy sum." Then, as a parting shot, he said, "Oh, tell me, which bit of tack was it that broke?"

'I said, "Tack? Broke? Captain Crump's tack would never break. It's always in absolutely perfect condition. No chance of anything breaking."

'The insurance chap shook his head. He said, "Are you really going to stick to that?"

'I said, "Of course I am. I've been with him since I was sixteen."

'Then he said, "Well, in that case I'm very much afraid that there is absolutely nothing we can do. If something had broken, you would have been able to sue the Captain. But in this case definitely no."

'So I lost a lot of money. But I didn't mind. I would never have lied about the Captain and his tack. As I said, unlike almost any other trainer in the country, it was always in perfect, safe condition. He valued his staff and his horses too much to allow anything else.'

The 1961–62 season was an *annus mirabilis* for Fulke Walwyn's brave little bay, Mandarin. He had an unbroken string of five victories, including a second Hennessy Gold Cup (the race founded by his owner's family firm) with 11 st 5 lb, the Cheltenham Gold Cup and finally and most triumphantly the Grand Steeplechase de Paris (the French Grand National).

On that day everything conspired to defeat Mandarin: the ground, which was always watered and had been further softened by scudding June rain; the condition of jockey, Fred Winter, who had been forced to waste hideously to make 9 st 10 lb for the four-year-old hurdler, Beaver II, later in the afternoon; the rubber bit which snapped in his mouth, as he landed after the third fence, leaving eight fences and 3½ miles of Auteuil's figure-of-eight course to be negotiated with neither brakes nor steering; and, finally, his patched-up legs, which gave out four fences from home. All these hazards Mandarin and Fred Winter overcame to beat the French horse Luminau by a rapidly dwindling short head. For the little crowd of English fans it was Agincourt, Trafalgar and Waterloo rolled into one. I had never seen or heard anything like the reception as Fred came wearily in with the bit hanging uselessly from his horse's mouth.

Ecstatic telegrams of congratulation flooded into Saxon House, Lambourn, from all over the world. The one which pleased Fulke most came from Middleham, from his old friend Neville Crump. It said simply, 'Why can't you buy yourself some decent tack?'

The headlines read: 'Gerry Scott put on the sideline by a

piece of cruel luck'; 'Scott's absence diminishes Northern scene'; 'Farewell to a great jockey'; 'Gerry Scott told to quit.'

Under the heading 'Thanks Neville Crump – Gerry Scott', this letter appeared in *Sporting Life*:

I have just learned . . . that my career as a jump jockey is over and I would ask the courtesy of your columns to pay a personal and warm tribute to Captain Neville Crump.

As I found out in an unbroken association of eighteen years, no jockey could wish for a more loyal, understanding and fair Guv'nor. I would like to add that no man could have a better friend.

I joined Warwick House as an apprentice in 1954 and had my first ride two years later. For the next sixteen years I've done my two and have had the good fortune to ride such outstanding chasers as Merryman II, Springbok, Much Obliged, Hoodwinked, Arcturus, Rough Tweed, Forest Prince and Rock's Cross.

It was after I had won the Grand National on Merryman II in 1960, following my victory on that superb jumper in the 1959 Scottish Grand National, that I broke my leg.

This was to happen another five times and I mention it in order to illustrate the Guv'nor's unswerving loyalty to me. . . .

. . . the Guv'nor never considered getting another jockey and directly I was fit, although possibly a little out of touch, he put me on the best horse in the yard.

. . . I owe many things to the Guv'nor over nearly twenty years and would like to express my deep debt to him and my privilege in working for him, a man who, like his horses, always does his best.

Gerry Scott
Middleham
Yorks

Neville replied,

My sincerest thanks to Gerry Scott for all the nice things he said about me in the *Life* on January 17th. I hope they were merited but a little loyalty does help in these dark and dreary days.

Talking about loyalty, what about Gerry himself? I have never had a more loyal friend and employee and if everyone behaved like him perhaps the world would not be in such a mess as it is today.

I am, naturally, extremely sorry that he has had to give up riding, but I am certain it is for the best as far as he is concerned.

It now only behoves everyone whom he has served so loyally to try and find him a job in racing.

No one has done more for the game, specially through his untiring efforts for the Injured Jockeys Association.

Thank you once again for everything, Gerry.

Looking back, Neville says, 'All my jockeys have been wonderful chaps and great friends. Johnny East was a splendid jockey and he too is a hell of a nice feller. That goes for my staff and for most of my owners as well over the years.'

As we heard from John Penny, Britain's longest-serving licence-holder has always held that it is easier to train the horses than the owners. On a recent occasion when dining with Lord Cadogan in a restaurant, he heard a woman owner, whose horses had been prevented through sickness from running, complaining bitterly in the most vitriolic terms about her trainer. Eventually Neville could stand it no longer. Although Lord Cadogan said, 'Sit down, Neville,' he refused. 'No, Bill, I've had enough. It's upsetting enough not to be able to run the horses, let alone have this sort of abuse.' He walked over to the strident woman's table. 'Madam,' he said, 'you may not have known that we were here, but Lord Cadogan and I couldn't help hearing everything that you have been saying. I shall be delighted for your horses to leave my yard first thing in the morning. As far as I am concerned you can stuff them right up. And I think I'd be right in assuming that there'd be plenty of room on either side!'

But with most of his owners Neville has had a good relationship, as he has with Lord Cadogan and Colonel Simon Lycett-Green. 'They are both my great friends and wonderful men,' he says. 'It was grand to win the Welsh Grand National for Lord and Lady Cadogan with their own home-bred Narvik. I have eight horses for them. Through Leslie Weaver I bought a mare in Ireland for only £600. She was called Freuchie, by Vulgan out of Nicotaina. Everything she has bred has turned out good. There was Voolin, For Good, Glen Lochan, who is a hell of a nice horse, and Lynemore, a splendid

172

four-year-old filly who has run only once and was second, beaten a length, to a top-class novice trained by the Dickinsons. It's great to win for people like that.'

Neville has had many good horses for more than a quarter of a century for Simon Green, including, of course, Rough Tweed, the great old favourite Whispering Grace, who won twenty-one races including ten on the flat, one of which was the November Handicap, and Even Melody, still thriving at the age of seventeen, but now officially retired with a score of thirty-three victories to his name and hunting on Exmoor.

Some idea of the relationship between Neville and his owners can be gained from the fact that when Judy Hay (the late Lady Bache Hay) was old and ailing, Neville and Simon came to the rescue. Neville says, 'Poor Judy was very old and she hadn't got a horse – something had happened to hers. So Simon offered her Even Melody and he won seven good races for her. She did terribly well with the old horse. The understanding was that Simon should have him back again when she died.'

Colonel Squeak Thompson was another old friend whose sense of humour did not desert him in a crisis. Neville says, 'The only time in my career that I was in trouble with the Stewards was over an authority to act on behalf of an absent owner. There was this fellow in Ireland – a member of the Turf Club – who said he had a decent horse that he wanted me to train for the Grand National, but when the time came to enter it, the owner was in hospital in America. So I sent a telegram in his name in order to enter the horse. I don't know to this day how anybody found out, but I was hauled before the Stewards at Cheltenham, one of whom was Colonel Thompson, and they fined me £50, as good as telling me I was a forger. A few weeks later we were racing at Newcastle and Squeak Thompson took me on one side to ask what I thought of their decision. "I think the Stewards are a load of shits," said I. "Fair comment," said he. "Let's go and have a drink."'

If Stewards know their job and do it properly, they are all right with Neville. But woe betide those who do not. One day at Liverpool some years ago when the local Stewards were short-handed, Lord Sefton instructed one of the underlings to ask Captain Crump whether he thought a certain elderly member of the nobility would be a suitable stand-in. Neville said, 'Of course. He's perfect. He can't see, he can't hear and knows fuck all about racing!'

What a record Neville's is. Three Grand Nationals; five Scottish Grand Nationals; two Welsh Grand Nationals; three Whitbread Gold Cups; the Topham Trophy two years running and the Grand Sefton Chase, both over the big Aintree fences; the Stones Ginger Wine Chase; the Hennessy Gold Cup; the Massey Ferguson Gold Cup; and the Mackeson Gold Cup.

The one place where Neville has enjoyed comparatively less success has been Chelterham. Cancello, who was tipped to win the Gold Cup and did indeed win the Mackeson, like many of Neville's horses, seemed to dislike the course. It has not been a truly happy hunting ground for the man who has won hurdle races, chases and flat races on almost every other course. Richdee, his current star, does not seem to like Cheltenham at all. The horse made a much bigger impact at Ascot, where he has won five of his six starts, but he has had recurring training problems and went lame for no apparent reason after running third in the Mackeson two years ago, after which he enjoyed a long rest.

It was at the start of Richdee's campaign last season, his first run since his lay-off, that his performance in the Timeform Handicap Chase at Ayr almost had his trainer in front of the local Stewards. Neville remembers it well. 'The truth was the old horse wasn't fit and he finished fourth to Hello Dandy, beaten quite a long way. The Stipendiary Steward wanted to hand me in, but, as I was staying with the Senior Steward of the meeting, this might have caused embarrassment and nothing was said. However, that evening my host asked how long I'd been schooling my horses in public and I told him. "Oh, for about forty-seven years!"'

Despite his somewhat fiery language and loud voice, you would have to go a long way to find a kinder, more unselfish man than Neville. His integrity is proverbial but he is no respecter of persons. He was outraged when the Jockey Club turned down applications from Fred Winter and other jumping trainers for a licence to train on the flat on the grounds that they did not have enough horses. So Neville applied for a licence himself, although he had only two potential flat runners. When his application was inevitably refused, he telephoned Weatherbys and asked, 'Do you know which owners I want to train for on the flat?' When the official said that he had no idea, Neville replied angrily, 'Lord Zetland and Lord Cadogan.' He told me delightedly, 'My flat licence arrived by return of post. Although I was happy to train for both noble lords, I had no flat horses for them! It was just that I was so disgusted by the injustice of the whole thing. And the fact that I got my licence immediately showed how utterly wrong the ruling was.' It was not long before the rule was changed. Once again Crump had seen justice done.

After a setback with the virus in the 1984–85 season, the winners have been coming from Warwick House again and prospects for the future look good. Neville, at seventy-five, is fitter than most men half his age. And the most loyal, most honest and, indeed, the most skilful trainer of our time has no intention of retiring. Heaven help the man who suggests such a thing. 'I'd like to have one more go with a good horse in the National,' he says. And it will be hard to find any more popular happening in the jumping world than a fourth Grand National triumph for Neville Crump.

Index

Abraham, Alex, 101
Aintree, 6–7, 32, 35–36, 66, 82,
   87–88, 91, 101, 104–105,
   113–114, 116
Aldbourne, 35
Aldershot, 12–24
Aldin, Cecil, 5
Alexander, Howard, 46
Ancil, Derek, 155–157
Anthony, Ivor, 6
Anthony, Jack, 6
Arkle, 65
Armstrong, Sam, 76, 86, 124
Armytage, Roddy, 165
Arnold, Matthew, 10
Ascot, 40, 64, 70–71, 174
Ashdown Forest, 3
Askew Family, 5
Askew, Gerald, 5, 37–38
Atkins, Dennis, 125
Ayr, 174
Ayr Gold Cup, 70, 101

Balliol College, 8–9, 167
Ballylinch Stud, 60
Barnard Castle, 59–60, 62, 67–68
Baroda, Maharajah, 76
Bates, Bobby, 100
Beary, Michael, 33–34
Beasley, Bobby, 157
Beasley, Harry, 157
Beaverbrook, Lord, 35
Bell, Ossie, 140
Beveridge, George, 140
Bicester, Lord, 33, 89, 94

Bird, Sir Alfred, 27–28
Bird, Sergeant-Major 'Dickie',
   24–25, 39–40, 44
Birmingham Handicap Chase, 113
Bissill, Jack, 78, 85
Blackshaw, Harry, 100
Bogside, 90, 139
Bonner, Harry, 65
Boulogne, 35
Boussac, Marcel, 105
Bradley, Sylvia Diana (Mrs Neville
   Crump), 27–30, 32–33, 35–41,
   45, 59–60, 68, 77–78, 97, 100,
   102, 107–108, 129–130, 151,
   164–165
'Braunshnaut, Baron Von', 14–16
Brignac, Comte Francois de, 105
Brogan, Barry, 95
Brogan, Jimmy, 94–95
Bromley, Peter, 144
Bronfam, Edgar, 101–102
Brooke, Betty, 59
Brooke, Geoffrey, 59, 61
Brooke, Capt. Peter, 101
Brookshaw, Tim, 141–142
Brotherton, Mrs, 104, 116, 155
Bruce, Sir Hervey, 86, 90–91
Buckfastleigh, 29
Buccleuch Hunters Chase, 139
Buckley, Pat, 162
Burstow Park Harriers, 3, 4
Butler, Rab, 145, 148

Cadogan, Lord, 164, 172, 175
Cambridgeshire, The, 72

Carlisle, 86, 88
Carlos-Clarke, Diana, 39
Carr, Arthur, 4
Carroll, Gerald, 109
Cazalet, Peter, 31–32, 91–92
Chambure, Comte de, 105
Château Renard, 47–48
Cheltenham, 39, 90–91, 100, 112, 125, 174
Cheltenham Gold Cup, 23, 65, 121, 122, 129, 131, 170
Chester Cup, 69, 72, 99
Claxton, Paddy, 78
Cockburn, Scotty, 24, 26
Colchester, 21–23
Collins, Ian, 57
Crump, Charles (father), 3–4, 7–9
Crump, Sarah (daughter), 59, 97, 106–107, 119–120, 128–130, 162–167
Cunard, Guy, 105
Cundell, Frank, 46, 48–50, 53–54, 56

Dante, 73–76
Dawnay, General Sir David, 40
Dawson, Tom, 68
Derby, 69–70, 72, 74–76, 142
Dewster, 'Dusty', 49
Dick, Dave, 117, 156
Dollar, Graham, 21
Dollar, Peter, 20–21
Doncaster, 6, 21, 60, 88, 91, 105, 122, 144, 152
Douglas, Jack, 144
Draper, Mr H., 130
Dreaper, Tom, 65, 88
Dufosee, Tony, 53
Dunkirk, 47

East, Johnny, 124–125, 127, 145, 152, 155, 172
Ebor, The, 72
Eclipse Stakes, 76

Evans, Gwyn, 65
Eve, Stephen, 24–25, 35
Exeter, 29

Farmiloe, Tom, 29
Fetherstonhaugh, 'Brud', 61
Fetherstonhaugh, Robert, 61
Field, Mrs, 59
Fitzwilliam, Lord, 57
Forster, Capt. Tim, 162
Fountain, Sergeant-Major, 54
Francis, Dick, 91, 103, 141
Fraser, Dr Alistair, 60
Freake, Sir Arland, 29
French Grand National, 37, 131, 170
Furlong, Frank, 31, 64
Furlong, Major Noel, 31

Gatwick, 5–6
Gibson, Joan, 109
Gibson, Laurence, 109
Gimrack Dinner, 105
Glanely, Lord, 72–73
Glendenning, Raymond, 89
Gloucester Hurdle, 39
Golden Miller, 32, 157
Goodfellow, Dawn, 102
Goodwood, 99
Gordon, Hector, 53, 56
Graham, Clive, 109, 144
Grand Military Gold Cup, 60
Grand National, 6–7, 23, 31–32, 42, 50, 53, 64, 66, 82–83, 87–104, 110, 113–119, 121, 139, 141–161, 173–175
Grand Sefton Chase, 174
Great Yorkshire Chase, 91, 152
Greenslade, 30
Gretton, Lord, 139
Guildford, 7

Haifa, 49–50, 52, 55
Hall, Harry, 69
Hall, Sam, 145

Hall, Sonny, 31–33, 35–36, 134
Hamey, Tim, 120
Hamer, John, 76
Hanbury, Ben, 31
Hanbury, Tom, 31
Handley, Roland, 77
Harper, Johnny, 79
Harrison, Claude, 114
Harrison, David, 21
Hart, Derek, 144
Hastings, Aubrey, 6, 110, 155
Hawkins, Colin, 122
Hay, Lady Bache, 173
Haydock Park, 29, 87–88, 91, 119,
   124–126, 153–154
Heath, Edward, 167–168
Henley, 9, 28, 165
Hennessy Gold Cup, 131, 166, 170,
   174
Hennessy, Mme K., 130
Herbert, Peter, 38, 54
Hislop, John, 89, 94, 154
Hobbs, Bruce, 6, 27, 39, 42–50,
   52–55, 57, 154
Hope, Lady Jane, 139–40
Houston, General, 15
Hudson, Robert, 63
Hunt, Sir John, 7
Hyde, Timmy, 66–67, 89

Irish Oaks, 71
Ironside, Field Marshal, Lord, 57
Irwin, Lord, 105
Isinglass, 60

Jenin, 50, 52–53
Johnston, Brian, 17
Johnston, Chris, 17
Joicey, Lord, 166–167

Karkur, 53–54
Kelso, 111, 140, 143
Kitson, Sir Timothy, 167

Lakeland, Ray, 144

Lamb, Ridley, 109–110
Lambie, James, 124
Lambourn, 21, 31, 170
Lambton, Hon. George, 70
Lancashire Chase, 7
Lane, Harry, 110–111, 115–116,
   119, 121
Limpsfield, 4, 7
Lincolnshire Handicap, 145
Linlithgow, Lord, 139–140
Lisley, Dawn, 59
Lisley, Jim, 59
Llewellyn, Sir Harry, 32
Lovat, Lord, 11–14
Ludlow, 38–39, 143
Lycett-Green, Colonel, 57, 166,
   172–173
Lyde, Colonel Wilfred, 79, 81
Lynn, Jack, 82

Magee, Sean, 37
Manchester, 62, 91
Mansur, 36–37, 39
Marlborough College, 7–8
Marseilles, 47, 49
Marsh, Alec, 156
Marsh, Sam, 5
Marshall, Bryan, 85, 104, 116, 119,
   122
Martyr, Major 'Tubby', 54
Massey Ferguson Gold Cup, 174
Mackeson Gold Cup, 174
McCalmont, Bunny, 60–62, 67
McCalmont, Dermot, 60–61
McCalmont, Colonel Harry, 60
McCalmont, Victor, 60–62,
   67–68, 101
McNaughton, Colin, 29
Merryman, 139–141, 145–147,
   149, 151, 153–158, 160–162
Middleham, 63, 68–69, 71, 73–74,
   76–77, 79, 81, 85, 97, 106, 110,
   127–128, 151, 162–163, 170
Mildmay, Lord, 31–32, 92–96,
   103–104

Molony, Tim, 84, 86, 119
Monger, Dennis, 144
Montague-Evans, Peter, 144
Morant, John, 66
Moraville, John de, 17, 20, 24
Morgan, Laurie, 154
Mount, Juliet, 61
Mundy, Mrs, 32
Murless, Sir Noel, 3, 63, 86,
    132–133, 164

National Produce Stakes, 72
Nelson, Lady, 6
Nelson, Peter, 76
Nevett, Billy, 74
Newbury, 62, 113–114, 116
Newmarket, 21, 31, 37, 60–62, 68,
    71, 74, 78
Newton Abbot, 29
Nicholson, Clifford, 82
Nicholson, David, 147, 166
Nicholson, 'Frenchie', 85
Nickalls, Colonel Tom, 116
Norfolk, Duke of, 63
Norrie, Lord Willoughby, 26
North Somerset Yeomanry, 39,
    41–44, 46, 49–50, 52, 57
Northumberland Plate, 69, 71,
    101
Nuffield, Lord, 39

Oaks, The, 72
Oaksey, Lord, 148
O'Brien, Vincent, 117–118, 121,
    141
Ohlson, Sir Eric, 73–74
Old Surrey Foxhounds, 3–4
Ollerton, 45–46
Oliver, Ken, 141
Osborne, John, 69–70
O'Sullevan, Peter, 109, 143
Owen, George, 127, 160
Oxford, 8–12, 14, 17
Oxford University Cavalry
    Squadron, 12–13, 15

Paget, Hon. Dorothy, 115, 118
Paget, Edward, 92
Palestine, 56–57
Palmer, Noel, 53
Payne, Bill, 53–55
Payne-Gallwey, Sir Philip, 162
Peacock, Dick, 71–72, 74–76, 130
Peacock, Dobson, 68–71
Peacock, Lenny, 75, 130
Peacock, Matthew, 71–79
Peel, Major Hugh, 7
Penney, John, 98–101, 103,
    132–133, 135–138, 172
Persse, Atty, 22, 31, 33, 59–61, 70,
    110, 132
Petre, Capt. Bobby, 67, 89
Pettifer, Tom, 53–55
Piggott, Ernie, 7
Piggott, Keith, 162
Piggott, Lester, 7, 124
Ponomarenko, Boris, 154–155,
    158
Powell Bay, 35
Power, Bobby, 65
Power, Jimmy, 104
Prakhov, Vladimir, 154–155, 157
Prendergast, Paddy, 3
Price, Ryan, 23, 84, 155
Prince of Wales Chase, 7
Prince Regent, 65–67, 88–89

Quinlan, Lenny, 76

Racecourse Association
    Steeplechase, 6
Radcliffe, Herbert, 123
Rank, J. V., 65, 98
Rayson, Tommy, 66
Reavey, Eddie, 92, 96
Redcar, 88, 90
Redhill, 5
Rees, Bill, 157
Renton, Bobby, 103–104, 116,
    155
Reynoldstown, 31, 64

Rhimes, Percy, 12, 14–15
Richards, Sir Gordon, 40
Rimell, Fred, 6, 110, 141,
  156–157, 159–160
Rosebery, Lord, 10, 63, 120
Roxburghe, Duke of, 111–112, 128

Sainsbury, Ivor (Lord), 101, 105
Sandown Park, 7, 113, 143
Scarborough, Earl of, 105
Scott, Gerry, 126–127, 140,
  144–146, 149, 152, 155, 159,
  162, 165–166, 168–172
Scottish Grand National, 90, 139,
  162, 171, 174
Scudamore, Michael, 118, 142
Sefton, Lord, 145–146, 156, 174
Shaw, Bernard, 11
Sheila's Cottage, 86–92, 95–100,
  103, 116
Sheppard, Gay, 151
Shone, Tommy, 104
Shortlands, 3
Sikorsky, General, 56
Smith, Bill, 85, 112, 119
South Oxfordshire Foxhounds, 9,
  12
South Oxfordshire Point to Point,
  16
Southwell, 84
Spence, Major Jimmy, 53
St. George, Ferris, 54
St. Leger, 70–71, 73–76
Stand Novices Hurdle, 67
Stanley Chase, 82
Stanton, Major, 54
Stayers Handicap, 90
Stockton, Lord, 10–11, 62
Stones Ginger Wine Chase, 174
Straker, Major Arthur, 101
Straker, Major Ivan, 101–102
Sutton, Major Dick, 163
Swindon, 31

Tatler, 4

Taylor, Joe, 70
Teal, 109–114, 116–118,
  120–121, 130, 141, 158,
  160–161
The 1000 Guineas, 73
The 2000 Guineas, 69, 72–73, 74,
  76
The Tetrarch, 60–61
Thirsk, 62, 122
Thompson, Arthur, 64, 78–83,
  85–88, 90–91, 95–98, 100,
  102–103, 105, 109–114,
  116–120, 122–124, 126–127,
  168
Thompson, Colonel, 7, 100, 173
Thompson, Enid, 85, 124
Thompson, Shirley, 124
Thrale, Peter, 16, 30
Tidworth, 12–13
Timeform Handicap Chase, 174
Topham, Mrs Mirabel, 115
Topham Trophy, 174
Torquay, 29, 37, 40
Totnes, 29
Towcester, 143
Townsend, Colonel Mouse, 56
Tremayne, Charles, 76
Tubbs, Reverend, 15
Turnell, Bob, 104
Tuxford, 46

Ulster Derby, 72
Ulster Grand National, 89
Upavon, 36, 38, 40, 46, 67, 78
Uttoxeter, 151

Vaux, Wing Commander, Peter,
  152, 163, 165
Vernon, John, 144
Victory Chase, 122
Victory Hurdle, 122

Wall, Peter, 67, 78
Wallace, Winifred, 139–141, 151,
  158

Walwyn, Fulke, 3, 31–32, 36–39, 91, 115, 120, 130, 147, 162, 170
Warden, Colonel Dick, 105
Warner, Ben, 29–30
Wavertree, Lord, 31
Weaver, Major Leslie, 139, 172
Wells, Somerset, 4
Welsh Grand National, 172, 174
Weston-Super-Mare, 41–42, 44
Wetherby, 81, 111, 169
Whaddon Chase, 10
Whalley, Sergeant, 54
Whitbread, Colonel Billy, 130
Whitbread Gold Cup, 130, 162, 174
Whiteman, Harry, 32, 92

Williams, Tom, 63
Williamson, 'Bluff', 128–129, 151
Willoughby de Broke, Lord, 105
Wilson, Gerry, 84
Wilson, Capt. Tom, 101
Wincanton, 143
Winter, Fred, 84, 98, 141, 155, 159, 170, 175
Woods, Oliver, 15
Worcester, 149
Wot No Sun, 101–104, 118–119, 161

York, 11, 20–21, 99, 105

Zetland, Marquess of, 105, 175